SPEAKING FOR THE MASTER

SPEAKING
FOR THE MASTER

A Study of Public Speaking for Christian Men

BATSELL BARRETT BAXTER

BAKER BOOK HOUSE
Grand Rapids, Michigan

THIS BOOK IS DEDICATED
TO
MY FATHER, BATSELL BAXTER
WHO HAS SPENT MOST OF HIS LIFETIME
IN HELPING TO TRAIN YOUNG PEOPLE
TO BE MORE USEFUL
IN THE SERVICE OF THE MASTER

Preface

FOR SEVERAL YEARS I have been aware of a pressing need for a textbook on religious speaking for use in Men's Training Classes among the churches. From time to time friends in widely scattered sections of the country have written to ask if there is such a book. Although there are scores of excellent textbooks, I know of none especially written to help train Christian speakers.

Within recent years it has become more and more apparent to me that the Lord needs more trained workers. The progress of Christianity depends, first of all, on its message. Next, it depends on the number and quality of its trained workers. God's messengers—whether they be preachers, teachers, elders, deacons, or others—need to be trained. In addition to knowing the message, they need to possess the skill by which that message may be effectively transmitted to others. Toward the accomplishment of that goal this book has been written.

It is designed for two kinds of use. It may be studied by individuals working alone, with profit to themselves and benefit to others. It is also especially suited for use in men's training classes, under the direction of a capable elder, or preacher, or teacher. The plan of the book follows the development of beginning speakers from the simple "first steps" on to the tasks of greater difficulty. The purpose of this study is twofold: to help the beginning speaker develop an understanding of what constitutes effective speech; and to help him learn to apply basic techniques to achieve individual improvement. Practice exercises have been included at the end of each chapter, for practice is absolutely essential in the development of speaking skill.

In writing this book I have drawn on all that I have learned in the speech field. The materials have come from many textbooks, from graduate seminars, from personal contacts with some of the leading speech people of our day, and from fifteen years' experience as a teacher of public speaking in the college classroom. I have borrowed generously, both consciously and unconsciously, from many sources. Whenever it has been possible to remember the original source, my indebtedness is indicated in the proper footnotes. In countless other instances the material has been so completely absorbed and made my own through years of classroom use that I do not know whom to credit. To such benefactors, known and unknown, I express deep gratitude. To William Norwood Brigance and to Alan H. Monroe, who have no peers in the speech field, I express the most profound appreciation; and I also wish to acknowledge indebtedness to Dale Carnegie, in whose writings were discovered a number of choice quotations.

I sincerely hope that classes can be arranged in many churches throughout the land so that a beginning can be made in training more *speakers for the Master*. For such classes, I would make the following suggestions:

(1) The ideal number for a class is from fifteen to twenty persons. The absolute maximum is thirty.

(2) One class meeting per week for sixteen to eighteen weeks is adequate. Meetings should be from one to one and one-half hours in length, and should be divided into a brief instruction period, followed by a longer practice period.

(3) Each person should have an opportunity to speak every week.

(4) The use of a good tape recorder throughout the course is recommended.

The cost in time, materials, and effort is not great; the results will live on into eternity.

BATSELL BARRETT BAXTER

NASHVILLE, TENNESSEE

Contents

CHAPTER I

The Importance of
Learning to Speak Well

WE LIVE IN an age when one of the most basic requirements for success in any field is the ability to speak well. Those who take the trouble to master the art of speaking are usually persons of influence and power. Every world leader has reached his place of eminence because he had the ability to talk and to persuade people to follow his ideas and ideals. Men in every walk of life find it necessary to have this same ability. "There is no other accomplishment," said Chauncey M. Depew, one-time president of the New York Central Railroad, "which any man can have which will so quickly make for him a career and secure recognition as the ability to speak acceptably." The executive, the banker, the doctor, men and women in business, all are called upon to express ideas effectively. It is important, therefore, in the most important work on earth—the Lord's work—that men and women be able to speak effectively.

Perhaps it is of some signficance that in the beginning God "spoke" the universe into existence. God's children have been

1

speaking ever since, and the most outstanding of all his children have been those who could speak most effectively for him. Noah, Moses, Joshua, the prophets, the apostles, and the Lord himself, all were speakers. From man's first recorded speech (Lamech's speech in Genesis 4:23–24) down through the centuries to the present hour, the ability to speak seems to have grown in importance. The first known textbook on speaking was written by Corax of Syracuse on the island of Sicily in the Greek period before Christ. Before 322 B.C. Aristotle had written his *Rhetoric*, which is still used in graduate schools throughout America. Today there are literally hundreds of textbooks on the art of speaking.

Frankly, good speech is more important to you than it was to your mother and father. It grows more important each year. Our forefathers faced the challenge of taming a new continent with gun, ax, and plow. Good speech was of little help. But now the frontier is gone. You don't need a gun to provide your food, and fewer and fewer of us use the plow. Today we use different, finer tools. Most of us sell our personalities, goods, or ideas through speech. With the coming of rapid transportation, the telephone, radio and television, our opportunities to speak for Christ have been multiplied a thousandfold. Speech has become so important in our twentieth century that more than 30,000,000,000 times a year we Americans cannot wait to see each other face to face but rush to speak to each other by telephone.

Lowell Thomas, famous radio commentator, has said: "As I look back at it now, if given the chance to do it all over again, and if obliged to choose between four years in college and two years of straight public speaking, I would take the latter, because under the proper direction it would include most of what one gets from a four-year liberal-arts course, and then some." This is probably overstatement, but it does emphasize the tremendous importance of speaking well. Bruce Barton, the New York advertising executive, added: "Face the situation frankly. Talkers have always ruled. The smart thing is to join them." Large department stores, the great industrial concerns, utility companies, insurance companies, all stress the importance of speech training for their employees. Labor organizations also offer courses in speaking. Hundreds of textbooks have been written, and hundreds of magazine articles published to tell men how to speak effectively. In high schools and colleges everywhere, and in adult classes in most cities, the art of speaking is taught.

THE LORD NEEDS SPEAKERS, TOO

In a world where there are so many who would pervert to selfish and base ends the God-given ability to speak, there is an urgent need for more trained Christian speakers. "The harvest indeed is plenteous, but the laborers are few: pray ye therefore the Lord of the harvest, that he send forth laborers into his harvest."[1] While much of the speaking that one hears —radio and television advertising, for example—suggests less loyalty to conviction and principle than to the sponsor who pays, good speaking requires a *good man* behind the words spoken, in the long run. Marcus Cato, the Roman, defined the ideal orator as "a good man speaking well," and there is some suspicion that he was repeating what the Greeks had said even earlier. In any case, Christians—good men—ought to be the foremost good speakers of every age.

Even though many see the need for more trained speakers in the Lord's work, there are only a few who are actually working to achieve greater skill in speaking. Perhaps it is because some do not realize that there are simple rules and

---

[1] Luke 10:2.

principles which, when mastered, will greatly increase their speech effectiveness. Perhaps it is not generally understood that old-fashioned speech training, which made oratory and declamation the basis of effective speaking, has passed. We do not orate today; we do not declaim. *We use the conversational style.*

The ideas suggested in this book have been discovered by careful observers down through the centuries to contribute toward effectiveness in speaking. They are practical common sense. There is nothing strange or difficult about them, and they can be mastered by anyone who *wants* to learn to speak more effectively for the Lord. In the Bible we are told that a master called his servants and delivered unto them his goods. To one he gave five talents; to another, two; and to another, one. *Notice that he gave everyone something.*[2] So it is with God. He has given every one of us certain abilities, and it is our responsibility to see that we do not "bury our talents."

All of us have the necessary equipment for speaking: teeth, tongue, lips, voice box, lungs. All of us have distinctive, individual styles. Each one of us has a personality accepted by our friends. We all have intelligence and are capable of ideas worthy of being heard by others. There is no reason why any one of us cannot be an effective speaker. Speakers are made, not born. As William Jennings Bryan said, "The ability to speak effectively is an acquirement rather than a gift." We can speak well if we want to, and we must for the Lord needs us. *We must learn to speak for the Master.*

INTENSITY OF DESIRE

Perhaps, here in the very beginning, it should be said that it costs more to go from New York to Los Angeles than to go

[2]Matthew 25:14–15.

from New York to Philadelphia. Or, more directly, you get out of a thing what you put into it. If you want to go a long way—really become a good speaker—you must do a lot of hard work. But the result will be worth more than what it costs. Perhaps the strongest single factor in determining whether you will be an effective speaker or not is the intensity of your desire. Several years ago I read a book by Napoleon Hill, entitled *Think and Grow Rich,* which set forth the secrets of success of the richest men in America. All together, these amounted to just one secret: "Want to become rich more than anything else in the world, and you will succeed." If you can achieve that same intensity of desire for the much higher purpose of *speaking for the Master,* your success will largely be assured.

ACTIVITIES

One of the goals of this class is to have every student speak every time it meets. There is no substitute for actual experience in speaking.

1. The first meeting of the class will be used for getting acquainted. Each person will stand and introduce himself to the group. In a brief speech not more than two minutes long, he should include the following information:
    a. Name (given slowly and distinctly, so that it can be remembered).
    b. Address.
    c. General background (where he is from, and so on).
    d. Type of work.
    e. Special interests of any kind.
2. As the course progresses, it will be of great value for each member of the class to know every other member by name. As the introductory speeches are made, each listener should impress on his mind the name of the speaker. At the end of the

introductions the instructor may well test the memories of various members of the class on the number of names recalled.

3. After each person has introduced himself and told his background, let the class make a brief sentence for each one, linking name and background, thus:

    a. John Bright (student)—"John is the brightest boy in his class at Central High."

    b. Bill Green (druggist)—"Green is the color of all one-dollar bills at the Southside Drugstore."

    c. Frank Holland (bus driver)—"Frankly, I do not wish to go to Holland on a bus."

4. In Appendix A you will find a "Case History Questionnaire." Fill it out carefully, and hand it to your instructor. It will guide him to your needs and will help you get the maximum amount of good from the course.

CHAPTER II

Stage Fright and
What to Do About It

"Racoon" John Smith began to preach after reaching manhood. His first sermon was of unusual interest to all who heard it, for in the midst of it he came abruptly to an embarrassing halt, floundered in an effort to go on, and then, realizing that there was an open door alongside the pulpit, fled unceremoniously into the night. Stumbling in the darkness he fell headlong, regained a degree of equilibrium, and had the courage to go back to the congregation and continue his sermon to its end. What brought on this strange behavior? He had stage fright.

Not only this pioneer preacher but almost every speaker before him or since has experienced stage fright in one form or another. Sometimes there is a trembling of the hands, arms, knees, or the whole body. Often there are a pounding of the heart, a rush of blood to the face, a shortness of breath, a trembling voice, with rising pitch or increased rapidity of speaking, and the terrible, terrible forgetting of what the person has planned to say. Some have described their feelings as "cold shivers running up and down the spine" or "hair standing on end." Always it is the same enemy: stage fright.

One biographer wrote of George Washington's first inaugural that he was so "visibly perturbed that his hand trembled and his voice shook so that he could scarcely be understood." Abraham Lincoln suffered from stage fright all his life. When he arose to speak, he "froze in his tracks" and he "had a far away prophetic look in his eyes." Even Cicero, who lived in the century before Christ, experienced stage fright and left us a record of his inner struggle in the words of Crassus: "I turn pale at the outset of a speech, and quake in every limb and in all my soul." It is said of Nathaniel Hawthorne that he was drenched in cold perspiration at the very thought of speaking at a banquet. John Dryden described his sensations: "Whenever I speak a cold sweat trickles down all over my limbs as if I were dissolving in water." The artist, the musician, the baseball star, the actor, the lover, the applicant for a job—all have the same dread malady and always have had. The hunter has "buck fever," and the modern radio personality has "mike fright"; but the malady is an ancient one.

Jon Eisenson[1] defines the problem as follows: "When an individual's pattern of responses is inadequate to meet a situation" he suffers stage fright. "Stage fright is a manifestation of an emotion—probably that of fear—arising out of difficulty in coping with the speech situation." The crux of the matter is that stage fright comes from fear that we are inadequate to meet a situation. Usually the chief element in this fear is an instinctive desire for the approval of others and a feeling that we shall not be able to win that approval. We are afraid of

[1]Jon Eisenson, *The Psychology of Speech* (New York: F. S. Crofts & Co., 1938), p. 264. Used by permission of Appleton-Century-Crofts, Inc.

failure, afraid that others will laugh at us, afraid of making a spectacle, afraid of not doing our best.

William Norwood Brigance describes the physical aspects of stage fright as follows:

Stage fright is not merely a mental state. It is also positively physical, for now enter the mysterious endocrine glands, especially the adrenal glands and possibly also the thyroid. When the impulse is sent to these glands, at once adrenalin (and possibly also thyroxin) is shot into the blood stream. At the same moment a trigger is pulled that dumps glycogen (a special form of sugar) from the liver into the blood stream. When these powerful secretions hit your heart, it starts to thump. When they hit the respiratory center in the brain, you start to gasp. When they hit the blood vessels going to the brain, they contract and you feel woozy. These are the obvious effects. Less obvious effects are even more profound. Blood is drawn away from the internal organs and transferred to outer muscles—arms, legs, etc.—and as a result the digestive process is slowed down or stopped altogether. . . . The blood clots more easily. Muscles become tense all through the body, and your tense throat muscles tend to produce a harsh and constricted voice. Salivary glands stop secreting, the mouth becomes dry, and you feel thick-tongued. In contrast, the sweat glands increase secretion, until beads of perspiration stand on your forehead and skin is moist. Breathing, of course, is difficult, for the breath stream is short and jerky. All of this takes place in the body of one who is afflicted by stage fright in its extreme form. In milder forms, the body undergoes a lesser amount of the same changes, and we feel "faintly sea-sick," have faint disagreeable sensations, or are simply keyed up and tense.[2]

---

[2]William Norwood Brigance, Speech: Its Techniques and Disciplines in a Free Society (New York: Appleton-Century-Crofts, Inc., 1952), p. 62. Used by permission of Appleton-Century-Crofts, Inc.

MASTERING STAGE FRIGHT

While it is of great value to understand thoroughly what stage fright is and what its causes are, our chief concern is what to do about it. Possibly you are now firmly convinced that you have all the symptoms, and that the situation is hopeless. Nothing is further from the truth, for stage fright can be cured.

Annoying and frightening as the above-named outward manifestations of stage fright are, they all can be made to vanish by removing the basic cause—fear. Fortunately, too, there are several simple and effective steps which will remove this fear.

1. **Choose an interesting subject.** Have you ever noticed how completely free from bashfulness a shy youngster becomes when he starts to tell about something that really interests him? He loses all fear when talking about baseball, or model airplanes, or a trip to summer camp. The same principle works with adults. Choose a subject that has been interesting to you, that often comes to mind, about which you like to converse, and about which you know something. You will be so interested in what you are saying that you will forget to have stage fright. Choose your own subject; better still, let your subject choose you.

2. **Master the subject thoroughly.** Much of the nervous tension in a speaker comes from fear that he will forget what he has planned to say. Sometimes it comes from knowledge that he has only a surface acquaintance with his subject and is not really giving his audience anything. In either case careful study will remedy the situation. Charles W. Lomas writes:

Many of these cases of severe stage fright are simply the result of inadequate preparation, sometimes without the student himself being aware of it. He may, for example, have simply memorized something that he has not made his own. The slightest distraction may destroy his set of cues, and he has not sufficient knowledge of the material to reconstruct them. Or he may have crammed his preparation into the period immediately preceding the speech class, or he may have tired himself by late hours in preparation the night before. To the student it will look as though sufficient time had been spent to insure mastery of the speech situation. But the same amount of time spread over several days would give him a far better grasp of his material and more assurance before the audience.[3]

Be sure that you have something worth while to say, and then be very sure that you have your outline firmly in mind. It is not good to try to memorize an entire talk. It is essential to know thoroughly the sequence of ideas that you plan to use. Memorize only your outline.

3. **Think about your subject and your audience, not about yourself.** There are primarily three places where a speaker's mind may rest while he is speaking: on his material, on the audience, or on himself. Good speakers largely forget themselves while concentrating upon their message and upon the way the audience is receiving it. It is almost always fatal to begin to think of yourself—how you are dressed, how correct your grammar is, how your gestures look, whether your speech is going over or not. "Forget self" is good advice in almost any life situation; it is doubly good in speaking.

4. **Use physical action while you speak.** It has been pointed out that, when stage fright takes hold of a speaker, certain glands exude adrenalin and other high-powered stimulants into his blood stream, physically preparing him to run or to fight; yet he must stand on the platform and speak. With all this high-

[3]Lomas,"Stage Fright," *Quarterly Journal of Speech*, 30:483.

octane fuel in his veins he is prepared for vigorous physical action, but he must stand still. Consequently his knees and hands tremble. He must use up this physical stimulus, and a good way of doing so is to move meaningfully about the platform, and to employ suitable gestures and body movements. Let the excess physical energy help you speak rather than hinder you in speaking. Deep and regular breathing, while you are still seated and after you have begun to speak, is another very valuable practice. In it all, try to relax. Consciously think of relaxing the muscles of the body. Mind has much influence over muscle.

5. **Remember that some nervous tension is necessary for good speaking.** Instead of regretting that you feel an extra nervous stimulus, be thankful for it, for it is a guarantee that you will not make a dull, listless speech. The very best speakers continue to feel such a stimulus even after years of experience, and they derive from it an urge and a zest that keep them from being listless and apathetic. Of course, practice has given them control of the tension, which they direct toward constructive rather than destructive ends. Instead of giving up to stage fright, use it as an aid toward the heights of good speaking.

6. **Speak at every opportunity, for experience builds confidence.** Nearly any new experience has the possibility of exciting fear. The way to remove this possibility is to transform new experiences into old ones as rapidly as possible. Nervous tension is felt most keenly in youth or at the first public appearances. After a few dozen appearances one's earlier apprehensions begin to seem rather ridiculous. They were not ridiculous at all—at the time—for until practice has created confidence a degree of uncertainty is natural. Do the thing you fear to do, and make a record of successful experiences. Accept every invitation to speak, for the more you speak the sooner speaking will be an easy and pleasant experience.

A SPECIAL RESOURCE FOR OVERCOMING FEAR

One who is using his talents in the Lord's work has every reason to feel perfectly confident that he is equal to every task that the Lord will set before him. The early chapters of the book of Exodus describe Moses as being so timid and fearful that he offers one excuse after another to persuade God not to call upon him for the great work that is to be done. Finally: " Moses said unto Jehovah, Oh, Lord, I am not eloquent, neither heretofore, nor since thou hast spoken unto thy servant; for I am slow of speech, and of a slow tongue. And Jehovah said unto him, Who hath made man's mouth? or who maketh a man dumb, or deaf, or seeing, or blind? is it not I, Jehovah? Now therefore go, and I will be with thy mouth, and teach thee what thou shalt speak."[4]

God made Moses as he desired him to be, and Moses was fully capable of doing the tasks that God gave him. So it is with us. God made us, and we are capable of doing what he desires us to do.

Let us with full confidence go forth to do whatever the Lord wants done. Stand erect, look the audience in the eye, believe in yourself, and then launch out to do whatever needs to be done. When David walked down across the valley to meet Goliath he fortunately forgot to think about himself and his own weaknesses and thought instead about the power of God and the job that needed to be done.

ACTIVITIES

1. In a brief speech give detailed directions for reaching a certain destination. Imagine that your hearers are strangers

---

[4]Exodus 4:10–12.

in the community and have asked help in finding the way to some scenic attraction, public building, or statue.

2. Make a brief speech on "My Most Embarrassing Experience."

CHAPTER III

Making Announcements

IN MOST WORSHIP services there comes a time when someone must stand up and make the necessary announcements, or notices. While it is desirable that the announcements be kept to the minimum, it is hardly possible to eliminate them. It is usually best to give them at a time when they cause the least break in the worship period, and to have a well trained person make them clearly, concisely, and emphatically. An ideal time is at the very beginning of the service: then they are out of the way, and provide no hindrance or interruption to the worship. Probably the next best time is immediately before the closing hymn and prayer.

The man who makes the announcements is more important than their place in the service. If he is nervous or poorly trained he can do almost irreparable damage to the spirit of worship. He should be at ease with people and before an audience. He should have better-than-average command of words, both in selecting and in pronouncing them. He should dress neatly but unobtrusively and should be as inconspicuous as possible.

ESSENTIALS FOR GOOD ANNOUNCEMENTS

By keeping certain simple essentials in mind, the maker of announcements will improve their quality immeasurably.

1. **Understand the facts.** How completely disturbing it can be when the announcer does not remember whether the special meeting is set for Tuesday evening or Thursday evening, and when he is not sure whether it will begin at 7:30 or 7:45. The very first requirement is to be sure—absolutely sure—of all facts.

2. **Understand the purpose.** What do you want the audience to understand? What do you want the audience to feel? What do you want the audience to do? Unless you have a clear conception of the purpose, your announcement is likely to be vague and lifeless: it will get little response.

3. **Emphasize the vital facts.** Special emphasis must be given to the key facts if they are to be remembered. One of the best ways to emphasize is through repetition. The Coca-Cola Company has spent millions of dollars to tell us over and over again about "the pause that refreshes." Other ways of securing emphasis are by increased or decreased loudness, by a pause or by raised or lowered pitch. The point is—emphasize the key facts.

4. **Speak so that all may hear and understand.** To the listener nothing is worse than to be able to hear a word here and there, but not to catch the gist of what the speaker is saying. In order for all to hear there must be *sufficient loudness* and *sufficient projection* of the voice. One auditorium had a permanent sign on the back wall, squarely facing the speaker: "Remember me on the back seat." In order to be understood, you must have good *articulation* and *enunciation*. How you may achieve these will be discussed in later chapters on voice production.

5. **Be brief.** Nearly always announcements take more time than is necessary. Careful preparation will be a great help. Ideally, the person making them should have them in hand the day before. If not a day, then at least an hour before.

ACTIVITIES

Below are several carefully chosen selections that will help you develop proper articulation and enunciation. By careful, daily reading aloud of these materials, before a thoughtful and cooperative listener, the average speaker will increase his skill almost unbelievably. Try it and see.

1. In evaluating a person's reading habits the following questions are often helpful:

   a. Is the voice pitched abnormally high or low?
   b. Is the voice quality harsh, metallic, nasal, unpleasant, or musical and pleasant?
   c. Is the tone thin and weak, or full and resonant?
   d. Is a lisp or hissed *s* detectable?
   e. Is the enunciation sufficiently sharp, or is it sloppy and muffled?
   f. Does the mouth open sufficiently wide with flexible controlled action of the lip muscles, or does the student talk "through his teeth" with little movement of the lip muscles?
   g. Are the vowel sounds chopped, sliced, or full and adequately prolonged?
   h. Does the breath flow easily and in sufficient duration for good phrasing, or is it so lacking in control that it breaks off at inopportune moments?
   i. Is a pattern of pitch tones repeated over and over, making for monotony, or is there considerable variation?
   j. Are unimportant words subordinated, or are all words

given nearly equal value, making it difficult for an audience to absorb the thought?
k. Is emotional expression present, or absent?
l. Does the speaker seem to give thought to what he is saying, or is he merely reading words?
m. Does the vocal expression indicate transition between thoughts, or does lack of transition cause monotony?
n. Does the speaker use an even pace or vary his timing?
o. Does the speaker rush his utterance, or does his basic speech rate permit his hearers time to absorb thought?
p. Does the speaker walk away with his conclusion?
q. Is the attitude of the speaker stiff and cold, or warm and friendly?

2. Practice selection containing all the basic sounds of the English language:

ARTHUR, THE YOUNG RAT

Once, a long time ago, there was a young rat named Arthur who could never make up his flighty mind. Whenever his swell friends used to ask him to go out to play with them, he would only answer airily, "I don't know." He wouldn't try to say yes, or no either. He would always shirk making a specific choice.

His proud Aunt Helen scolded him. "Now look here," she stated. "No one is going to aid or care for you if you carry on like this. You have no more mind than a stray blade of grass."

That very night there was a big thundering crash, and in the foggy morning some zealous men—with twenty boys and girls —rode up and looked closely at the fallen barn. One of them slipped back a broken board and saw a squashed young rat, quite dead, half in and half out of his hole. Thus, in the end the poor shirker got his just dues. Oddly enough his Aunt Helen was glad. "I hate such oozy, oily sneaks," said she.

3. Practice sentences emphasizing certain sounds (those, after the opening, indicated by a capital letter):

  a. I Eat all I sEe that is appealing.

  b. If Any one of the mAny here is Interested he may re-Enter the haunted house.

  c. Old Age will allAy the fears which the inability of juvenile thinking may arrAy as being unmistAkably impossible.

  d. LEt the Egg hatch first.

  e. At last, the immAculately dressed mAn came to the bAnquet.

  f. After Tanya had Asked to be introduced to the master, she pAssed by quickly.

  g. FAther was cAlm throughout the alArming display.

  h. The clOth had been eaten by mOths.

  i. He clAWed and scratched, and the AWful sound of his cries was distressing to his mother-in-lAW.

  j. As many as will Obey may be said to follOw and to enjoy the fellOwship of others.

  k. She put the wOOlen skirt away and tOOk out the one which would be cooler.

  l. The water OOzed into the canOE where the hole had been punched by the fOOlish lad.

  m. The sUn seemed dOUbly bright to Us that morning.

  n. About the momEnt he had summOned enough courage to volunteer, a shot sounded which scared him Again.

  o. EARly in the morning the gIRl returned to bring the fUR coat to the tailor.

  p. The tailOR took down the pattERn in order to make an effORt to measURe for size.

  q. The bOY stepped in the OIl and became very an-nOYed.

    r. In his aroused Ire he threw the pIe into the fIre.

    s. The EArache made him wEAry and caused him to appEAr fatigued.

    t. ThERE, as she descended the stAIR, the hEIRess was cAREful to make the proper appearance.

4. Practice sentences emphasizing consonant sounds:

    a. There were Several poliCemen near the houSe.

    b. The great Zone of deSert land is alwayS barren.

    c. A WHispering campaign will spread a story every-WHere.

    d. After she looked out the Window she Walked slowly aWay.

    e. I THink a faiTHful friend is worth more than anything.

    f. If THey go togeTHer I may go wiTH THem.

    g. The SHip waSHed aSHore to cruSH itself on the rocks.

    h. He was tricked by the illuSion of a miraGe.

    i. A CHance remark of a teaCHer can cause muCH trouble.

    j. The Giant enGine is supported by a huGe under-carriaGe.

    k. That Town is in a beauTiful valley to the wesT.

    l. In the Dark meaDow he hearD the call of a lonely birD.

    m. Most of the coMpany had left before we caMe.

    n. That is Not sufficieNt reasoN for his actioN.

    o. The riNGiNG chimes played the tune of an old soNG.

    p. The Lake in the moonLight Looks cooL and inviting.

    q. He Hurt His shoulder on the jutting rocks overHead.

    r. He Finally lauGHed and walked oFF without a word.

    s. On the Very edge oF the riVer there is a large caVe.

    t. I Can't go now beCause I must read this booK.

    u. The Game was just beGinning when his leG was injured.

    v. If one Puts aPples in a cool Place they stay fresh.

    w. The Boy managed to kill a raBbit with a cluB.

5. Tongue twisters and other exercises for developing flexibility of the tongue and lips:

    a. Peter Piper, the pepper picker, picked a peck of pickled peppers. A peck of pickled peppers did Peter Piper, the pepper picker, pick. If Peter Piper, the pepper picker, picked a peck of pickled peppers, where is the peck of pickled peppers that Peter Piper, the pepper picker, picked?

    b. Theophilus Thistle, the thistle sifter, sifted a sack of thistles with the thick of his thumb. A sack of thistles did Theophilus Thistle, the thistle sifter, sift. Theophilus Thistle, the successful thistle sifter, in sifting a sieve full of unsifted thistles, thrust three thousand thistles through the thick of his thumb.

    c. Six long slim slick slender saplings.

    d. Algy met a bear. The bear was bulgy, and the bulge was Algy.

    e. Ten tiny toddling tots testily trying to train their tongues to trill.

    f. Around the rugged rock the ragged rascal ran.

    g. Susan sells sea shells on the seashore.

    h.
        La—lei—le—li—lo—lu,
        Na—nei—ne—ni—no—nu,
        Da—dei—de—di—do—du,
        Ta—tei—te—ti—to—tu,
        Ra—rei—re—ri—ro—ru,
        Ba—bei—be—bi—bo—bu,
        Ma—mei—me—mi—mo—mu,
        Pa—pei—pe—pi—po—pu,
        Wa—wei—we—wi—wo—wu,
        Sa—sei—se—si—so—su,
        Za—zei—ze—zi—zo—zu.

6. Typical church announcements for practice:

    a. We wish to welcome those of you who are visiting with

us today, and to extend to each of you a cordial invitation to return whenever possible.

b. We regret to announce the serious illness of Mrs. Raymond Mathews, who is a member of this congregation. She is in Room 4024 of the Mid-State Hospital. Although no visitors will be permitted for a few days, we are sure that our prayers, cards, and flowers will be appreciated.

c. On Tuesday evening the young people of high-school and college age will make a visit to the Rest Haven Home for the Aged. A brief worship service will be conducted for these elderly people, most of whom are permanent shut-ins. The young people will meet at 7:00 o'clock at the church building.

d. Remember the regular schedule of services for the coming week. The sermon subject for the 7:30 Sunday evening service will be "God's Purpose for Man." Prayer meeting will be conducted at 7:30 on Wednesday evening. You have a special invitation to attend both these services.

CHAPTER IV

Reading the Bible

NOTHING IS MORE vital in a worship service than the effective reading of the Bible, for when the scriptures are read God speaks to men. Yet the Bible is often read in a careless and thoughtless way that fails to keep the attention of the congregation. As a consequence the reading is often relegated to a minor place in the worship service. It is somewhat reassuring to find that even in this twentieth century many Sunday worship services in England include the reading of an entire chapter from the Old Testament and another from the New Testament. Not only is there a need for greater attention to the public reading of the Bible, but there is a need for more training in oral reading because of the great value it has in family worship and in personal devotional study. It would be difficult to find a more beautiful picture than a family—father, mother, and children—seated around the fireplace in the living room with the father reading to the family from the open Bible.

One who aspires to read the Bible in public should provide himself with a volume, containing both Old and New Testaments in a clear, distinct type practical for public reading. It should be a sturdy book that will endure long and constant use. The King James (Authorized) Version or the American Revised Version is a wise choice so far as the text is concerned. The King James Version is probably the more beautiful and has the advantage of being the one most familiar to the average hearer. The American Revised is more accurate, and its wording is more in accord with present usage, yet it keeps the sacred style and sound—factors which remind the listener that the Bible is a sacred book. Translations in modern speech should be used only to supplement these basic versions.

HISTORICAL SKETCH OF BIBLE READING

The public reading of the Bible is an ancient custom. In the long ago Joshua assembled the entire population of Israel in the natural amphitheater between Mt. Ebal and Mt. Gerazim in Samaria, and "read all the words of the law, the blessing and the curse, according to all that is written in the book of the law. There was not a word of all that Moses commanded, which Joshua read not before all the assembly of Israel, and the women, and the little ones, and the sojourners that were among them."[1] Every successive reformation was associated with the public reading of "the Law." In the time of Nehemiah and Ezra, "they read in the book, in the law of God, distinctly; and they gave the sense, so that they understood the reading."[2] In the synagogues, with their public reading of the scriptures, the whole law was read in about three or three and a half years. At Nazareth, Jesus entered into the synagogue on the Sabbath day, as his custom was, and stood up to read the appointed lesson of the day.[3]

The assemblies of the early Christians often centered around

---

[1]Joshua 8:34–35.
[2]Nehemiah 8:8.
[3]Luke 4:16–30.

the reading of the scriptures. As Justin Martyr wrote, in "The First Apology":

> And on the day called Sunday, all who live in cities or in the country gather together to one place, and the memoirs of the apostles or the writings of the prophets are read, as long as time permits; then, when the reader has ceased, the president verbally instructs, and exhorts to the imitation of these good things. Then we all rise together and pray.[4]

The poverty of the early Christians, the great cost of manuscripts, and the inability on the part of many in the early church to read, made frequent reading of the scriptures a necessary part of the service.

For fifteen hundred years there was no printed Bible. The manuscripts were copied and recopied, and worn out by frequent use. Even as late as Shakespeare, a Bible was worth as much as a good-sized farm, and few could own the complete scriptures. The Bible was often chained to a lectern or desk, so that devout persons might read at various hours of the day. No doubt readers would often volunteer to read aloud to groups of persons. Possibly in this way Shakespeare gained his knowledge of the Bible.

IMPORTANCE OF BIBLE READING

In addressing a group of young ministers, William M. Taylor said:

> The reading ought not to be subordinate to your sermon, but your sermon ought to be subordinate to it. Indeed, the end of your preaching will be secured, in a large measure, when you have stirred up the hearers to search the Scriptures . . . but if, in your public treatment of the Word of God, you are listless and mechanical, you cannot hope to interest any one in the study of it. The eloquent

---

[4]Justin Martyr and Athenagoras, *Writings,* transl. by Dods, Reith, and Pratten, p. 65.

McAll, of Manchester, England, is reported to have said: "If the Lord had appointed two officers in His Church, the one to preach the Gospel and the other to read the Scriptures, and had given me the choice of these, I should have chosen to be a reader of the inspired Word of God," and with such an opinion, we are not surprised to learn that he excelled in that exercise; nay, it is not improbable that his deep reverence for the Bible, so manifested, contributed largely to the power of his discourses.[5]

Because the reading of the scriptures is God's way of speaking to men, the reader has a sacred responsibility to read correctly and well. The reading of the Bible must in some sense mean the interpretation of the Divine Spirit and Will to the hearts of men. As S. S. Curry writes:

A man may stand upon a high mountain and with a little glass throw a reflection of the great sun to the valley below. The little flash of light may carry a message to his friends, or be a signal to a far-off garrison. So the individual soul may reflect the Sun of suns. A reader can reflect by the voice to other souls the life of the Divine. The little mirror may seem totally inadequate, but it can reflect the sun. When the Bible is read with genuineness and simplicity, no art is more sublime, nothing moves more deeply the hearts of a congregation.[6]

Securing a person qualified for so exalted a work as the reading of the Bible is not easy. As Francis G. Peabody said:

What are the qualifications for . . . reading? They are of two kinds. On the one hand are the untaught gifts of discernment, refinement, wisdom, self-effacement, sympathy. No professor of elocution can make an effective Bible-reader out of a light-minded, consequential, self-assertive, or sentimental man. Reading is an extraordinary revelation of character; and it would surprise many a

⁵Taylor, *The Ministry of the Word,* p. 220.
⁶Curry, *Vocal and Literary Interpretation of the Bible,* pp. 12–13.

minister to be told with what precision his reading of the Bible betrayed affectation, or hardness, or indolence, or conceit. On the other hand, there are many traits of effective Bible reading which can be easily acquired by a teachable man. He can be saved from artificiality, corrected in blunders, disciplined in a rational use of the voice, restrained from employing the nose or throat as organs of expression, and, more than all, encouraged to take pains, and to be ashamed of appearing before his congregation with a Bible passage unstudied, haltingly delivered, or misunderstood.[7]

UNDERSTANDING THE BIBLE

It should be obvious that a person can do little to lead others to an understanding of a passage of the scriptures until he himself understands its message. Following are several simple questions which will aid in understanding the Bible:

1. **To whom was the passage written?** The Bible consists of sixty-six separate books, written over a span of more than sixteen hundred years. Various sections have primary application to the patriarchs, or to the Hebrew nation, or to the apostles, or to Christians in general. It is important to know about any passage whether it deals with the Patriarchal Age, or the Mosaic Age, or the Christian Age. Only one who thus "rightly divides the scriptures" can hope to understand them.

2. **Who is speaking?** Not only the Lord but, from time to time, others speak in the pages of the Bible. Job's wife urges her distraught husband to "curse God and die," but this is hardly the "word of God." The devil speaks; human beings express their views; the Lord speaks. Obviously, a reading of the context is necessary before one can properly evaluate what is spoken.

3. **What is the design of the passage?** Is it a simple narrative? Is it a prophecy? Is it a command? Is it figurative? Is it lit-

---

[7]As quoted in *ibid.*, pp. xvi–xvii.

eral? Only by understanding the general design, or purpose, of the passage can one properly understand the specific message.

In reading the Bible to others one should lay aside private theories and prejudices, for these prevent that teachable attitude toward the Bible which is the first essential to genuine feeling and true natural expression. The reader's attitude must be: "Speak, Lord, thy servant heareth."

READ NATURALLY AND SIMPLY

After a thorough understanding of the passage, the next fundamental has to do with a natural, genuine, simple style of reading. One of the greatest hindrances to effective reading of the Bible is the assumption of an artificial "holy tone." Carelessness or slovenliness on the one hand and an excess of art on the other are twin enemies of good reading. S. S. Curry's suggestions are helpful along this line:

Imagine that you are called to read a letter from a mother to a son who is blind. Will you endeavor to exhibit your elocutionary powers, your fine pronunciation, your superior understanding? Will you endeavor to charm and fascinate one who is thinking, not of you, but of his mother, or seek to gain his attention by peculiar technical inflections, so as to project into the words of the mother meanings peculiar to yourself? As you look into that serious face, you remember that the letter will touch deeper chords than you can reach. There are ties between that blind boy and his mother with which you have nothing to do. With the utmost simplicity, with the most direct truthfulness, with as little as possible of your own personal experience, with less of your own personal expression than ever before, you will seek to transmit to the boy the message which to him is sacred.[8]

Dwight L. Moody, the widely known evangelist, told the story of a father and a son who became estranged. The son left

---

[8] *Ibid.*, p. 14.

the home in hot anger and went West. Years later the father said to a friend who was going West, "If you ever find my son, tell him I still love him." The friend finally found the son in a gambling den, told him he had a message from his father, and called him out where they would be alone. The boy was scowling, for he expected to hear that he had been disinherited. The man said, "Your father told me to tell you that he still loves you." That brought the son around. He softened and returned home.

How would you deliver that sentence? In a loud harsh voice? In an effort to imitate the father? No, you would deliver it quietly, simply, and earnestly.

CHIEF TYPES OF BIBLICAL MATERIAL

For the development of skill in public reading it is helpful to divide the scriptures into their basic types. The following divisions are patterned in general after those of Curry:

1. **Narrative**—"the telling of a story." The ability to tell a story requires what is generally called historical imagination—the ability to visualize the original situation and the characters, and feel as they felt. It is helpful to know the customs and dress, the geographical scene, and the times. A story should have spirit and life, and the fundamental event or object must be so vividly portrayed that the subordinate parts will be thrown into the background. Suggested passages for practice: (a) the account of the flood, Genesis 6, 7, and 8; (b) the story of Naaman, II Kings 5; (c) the story of Christ's birth, Luke 2; (d) Paul's voyage to Rome, Acts 27 and 28.

2. **Didactic**—"that which is intended to teach or instruct." Because the main purpose of didactic passages is in the vein of teaching, explanation, and instruction, they are primarily intellectual. They appeal to the reason rather than to the emotions or feelings. The chief obligation is to make the thought

clear. Suggested passages for practice: (a) the Proverbs of Solomon; (b) Romans 12; (c) I Corinthians 11:17–34; (d) James 2:14–3:12.

3. **Oratory**—"that which was delivered originally as a public speech." One of the main factors distinguishing this type of passage from others is its depth of conviction. Usually there is deep feeling and strong emphasis. The style of reading should be conversational, but it must also have strong emphasis in order to show the deep convictions. The style must also be direct and personal. Suggested passages for practice: (a) Joshua's farewell address, Joshua 24; (b) Christ's sermon on the mount, Matthew 5, 6, and 7; (c) Peter's sermon on Pentecost, Acts 2:14–36; (d) Paul's speech in Athens, Acts 17:22–31.

4. **Allegory**—"that which contains, in a figurative story, a meaning metaphorically implied but not expressly stated." The parables of the Lord fit into this classification. In them, Jesus gave simple, understandable stories which had a deeper, spiritual meaning for hearers mature enough to understand them. Allegorical speaking also serves to present some more or less abstract truth in vivid, objective form where it can be remembered more easily. Suggested passages for practice: (a) II Samuel 12:1–7; (b) Ecclesiastes 12:1–8; (c) Matthew 13; (d) Galatians 4:21–31.

5. **Dialogue**—"that which, whether in prose or verse, portrays life or character by means of dialogue and action." Many times the scriptures resort to conversation to present truth vividly and interestingly. The reader of such passages does not try to impersonate the actual speakers with action and voice, but rather *suggests* their personalities by moderate voice changes. Suggested passages for practice: (a) Genesis 3; (b) II Chronicles 10; (c) the book of Job; (d) Mark 12:13–34.

6. **Poetry**—"that which, whether actually sung or not, is generally composed in stanzas, is expressive of the poet's feeling

rather than of outward incidents or events." This type of passage reflects the deepest and strongest feelings of the human heart. It requires the reader to enter into the mood and communicate it to his hearers by inflection, voice quality, rhythm, and rate. The poetic passages of the Bible are to be read more slowly and deliberately than other passages. Suggested passages for practice: (a) Exodus 15:1-19; (b) the book of Job; (c) the Psalms; (d) the Song of Solomon.

COMMON FAULTS IN READING

Among the common faults in public reading of the Bible are the following:

1. Inadequate preparation.
2. No introduction.
3. Failure to comprehend the thought.
4. Lack of sincerity.
5. Failure to note punctuation.
6. Too much bodily activity.
7. Losing the place.
8. Unfamiliarity with the house.
9. Untrained voice.
10. Too fast.

ACTIVITIES

1. Let each member of the class choose a Biblical passage from ten to fifteen verses long, study it with care and practice reading it aloud, and then present it before the class.

2. After each presentation, let the members of the class use the materials of this chapter under the guidance of the instructor to evaluate the reading in an instructive and helpful way.

CHAPTER V

Teach Us to Pray

ANOTHER SPEAKING ACTIVITY in which Christian men are often called to engage is the leading of public prayer. In some respects this is more difficult than making announcements or reading of the Bible. On one occasion the apostles came to Jesus with the request, "Lord, teach us to pray."[1] These mature religious men felt an urgent need to learn more about prayer. It is right that we, too, should study the art of framing an acceptable prayer. In our day there are few men who do not need to study prayer and especially to study the art of leading effective, scriptural public prayers. No better place can be found to begin the study than Jesus' answer to his disciples.

WHEN YE PRAY

And when ye pray, ye shall not be as the hypocrites: for they love to stand and pray in the synagogues and in the corners of the streets, that they may be seen of men. Verily I say unto you, They have received their reward. But thou, when thou prayest, enter into thine inner chamber, and having shut thy door, pray to thy Father

---

[1] Luke 11:1.

who is in secret, and thy Father who seeth in secret shall recompense thee. And in praying use not vain repetitions, as the Gentiles do: for they think that they shall be heard for their much speaking. Be not therefore like unto them: for your Father knoweth what things ye have need of, before ye ask him. After this manner therefore pray ye: Our Father who art in heaven, Hallowed be thy name. Thy kingdom come. Thy will be done, as in heaven, so on earth. Give us this day our daily bread. And forgive us our debts, as we also have forgiven our debtors. And bring us not into temptation, but deliver us from the evil one. For thine is the kingdom, and the power, and the glory, for ever. Amen.[2]

In the foregoing text the following principles stand out:

1. **We must not pray to be seen of men.** In order to be acceptable a prayer must be designed for the ears of the Lord rather than the ears of men. At this point the average Christian man faces one of his severest tests. It is so difficult to stand before a congregation of people and frame a prayer that is appropriate for the entire group, yet almost forget that the audience is present. The speaker's attention is likely to dwell on matters of grammar, sentence structure, word choice, appropriateness of the ideas expressed, and above all on what people will think of the prayer, whereas all of these things should be pushed completely out of the mind. A successful public prayer can be led only when the leader's mind is filled with the needs of the people and of voicing these needs to the all-powerful, loving heavenly Father who can and will help them.

2. **We must not use vain repetitions when we pray.** The meaningless repetition of certain set words and phrases is an abomination to the Lord. It simply means that the one who uses them has "turned off his mind" without "turning off his

---

[2]Matthew 6:5–13.

tongue." Although any word pattern may be thoughtfully prayed, it is extremely likely that the timeworn expressions which follow have lost their meaning for most of us: "Our all-wise and ever-to-be-adored heavenly Father," "We pray not for ourselves alone but for all those for whom it is our duty and our privilege to pray, the world over," "Bless thy ministering servants everywhere," "Finally save us, if we have been found faithful to the end, and we will give thee all the praise, for it is enough." These, and other similar expressions, need to be used more thoughtfully and only when we are sure that t! ₂y say exactly what we want to say to the Lord. Repetition is not wrong. In the parable of the importunate widow (Luke 18), Christ encourages us to continue to call upon the Lord for what we need; but there is never any place for *vain repetitions.*

3. **We must follow the pattern of the model prayer.** The prayer that Christ used in teaching his disciples to pray is not a set ritualistic form to be repeated over and over, but a perfect model of what our prayers should be. It is a model in its *brevity,* for it contains only sixty-nine words and can be spoken in less than a minute. It is a model in its *scope,* for it deals with both spiritual and physical concerns. It is a model in its *simplicity,* for there is no word in it that a child would fail to understand. It is a model in its *directness,* for there are no vague, high-flown expressions.

THE MODEL PRAYER

"Our Father who art in heaven." The prayer is addressed to God, the creator of the universe, but with the emphasis upon his fatherhood and hence his concern for his children.

"Hallowed be thy name." The second element of the prayer is that of praise and adoration to God. Too many prayers are almost exclusively filled with requests for God's blessings.

Much, much more of praise and adoration is needed in our prayers.

"Thy kingdom come." When Jesus taught his disciples this prayer the kingdom, the church, had not yet come. This phrase must undoubtedly include his deep concern that the plans for the establishment of the church on Pentecost be carried out without hindrance. In its deeper and more permanent meaning, the phrase expresses the desire that Christ's kingdom come into the hearts of all men and to all continents throughout all time. In this broader sense it is still appropriate for Christians to pray, "Thy kingdom come."

"Thy will be done, as in heaven, so on earth." After three statements regarding heavenly things, the prayer devotes the remaining four to matters of this earth. The person who sincerely prays this part of the prayer is committing himself to follow the Lord's will in the complete manner in which the angels of heaven follow it.

"Give us this day our daily bread." The request is only for the necessities of the day. It implies the Christian view of life. No anxiety for the morrow; no thought for the luxuries and extravagances of the world.

"Forgive us our debts . . ." Luke 11:4 has, "Forgive us our sins . . ." This is confession of wrong and implies a penitent spirit. Without such humility no prayer can be acceptable.

"Lead us not into temptation . . ." This is a request for God's help in the greatest undertaking of our lives—that of being eternally saved.

"For thine is the kingdom, and the power, and the glory, for ever." Again comes the recognition of the greatness of Jehovah, with implied reverence and adoration.

"Amen." The literal meaning is, "So be it." This has long been the acceptable means of concluding a prayer. Here it receives the Lord's approval.

CONTENTS OF AN ACCEPTABLE PRAYER

From the foregoing and from the study of other scriptures concerning prayer we can conclude that an acceptable prayer should include the following:

1. **Address to God.** Nowhere in the scriptures is there a prayer addressed to "Mary, the blessed mother of Jesus," to "St. Anne," to "St. Christopher," or to others. If we follow the Bible, we will pray only to God.

2. **Praise.**

3. **Thanksgiving.**

4. **Confession.**

5. **Petitions.**

6. **"In the name of Christ."** When Jesus was upon the earth it was not possible to pray through him to the father; but, once he ascended to heaven, it became necessary for our prayers to be offered through his name. The apostle Paul speaks of Jesus as the "mediator between God and men."[3] Just before he was ready to leave the earth, Jesus said: "If ye shall ask anything in my name, that will I do."[4] He also said: "Verily, verily, I say unto you, If ye shall ask anything of the Father, he will give it you in my name. Hitherto have ye asked nothing in my name: ask, and ye shall receive. . . . In that day ye shall ask in my name. . . ."[5]

THE MAN WHO PRAYS

Not only are there certain requirements for the prayer itself; there are certain very definite requirements for the man who leads the prayer:

1. **He must be a Christian.** "If ye abide in me, and my words abide in you, ask whatsoever ye will, and it shall be done

---

[3]I Timothy 2:5.
[4]John 14:14.

[5]John 16:23, 24, 26.

unto you."[6] "We know that God heareth not sinners. . . ."[7] "The supplication of a righteous man availeth much in its working."[8]

2. **He must be a spiritually minded man.** In the delicate act of leading others in prayer, it is helpful if the leader be a man of much prayer and, therefore, of intimate acquaintance with the Lord. Long years of earnest communion with God through prayer prepare one best for the difficult act of leading public prayers.

3. **He must believe in prayer.** "But let him ask in faith, nothing doubting: for he that doubteth is like the surge of the sea driven by the wind and tossed."[9] "And all things, whatsoever ye shall ask in prayer, believing, ye shall receive."[10]

4. **He must desire that the will of God be done.** Jesus is our example in this as in everything else. When in the agony of Gethsemane, he prayed, "My Father, if it be possible, let this cup pass away from me: nevertheless, not as I will, but as thou wilt."[11]

5. **He must speak for the congregation.** In public prayer, one man *leads* the prayer for the entire congregation to follow. It is obvious that he must take into consideration the needs and feelings of the group whose minds he leads. He must say the things that are appropriate for the entire group to say. Furthermore, he must speak loudly enough for all to hear and distinctly enough for all to understand. Else how can they follow?

ACTIVITIES

1. Read these sample prayers,[12] and evaluate them:

a. Merciful Father, help us to remember that our sojourn here is brief and that in the twinkling of an eye we may be called. . . .

6John 15:7.
7John 9:31.
8James 5:16.
9James 1:6.

10Matthew 21:22.
11Matthew 26:39.
12Showalter and Cox, *A Book of Prayers,* pp. 22–55.

Grant that we may study thy word earnestly and sincerely and allow the same to direct us. We recall with sadness our past weaknesses. Henceforth, help us to be stronger. Bless, we beseech thee, the ministers of thy word. May their lives be pure, their speech sound and their hearts tender. Bless the fathers and mothers of our land that they may be strong to bring up their children in thy nurture and admonition. Bless the rulers of our fair country and all that are in high places; that we may lead a tranquil and quiet life in all godliness and gravity. Bless our friends, our enemies if such we have, our kindred, and all for whom we should pray—bless them, Father, in accordance with thy wisdom, power, and infinite compassion. May all men come to know that the best thing in life is pure and undefiled religion. Equip us for battle. Prepare us to live. Comfort us in sickness and in death. Give us an eternal home with thee. In the name of him that loved us, and loosed us from our sins by his blood. Amen.

b. Our Father who art in heaven, hallowed be thy name. . . . It is with a sense of deepest gratitude, of conscious guilt, and of utter helplessness that we come into thy presence. May our guilt be lost in thy tender mercy and our weakness in thy marvelous strength. In the morning of life, may we hear the divine call. May we give unto thee the first fruits of our earthly existence. Help us to love thee supremely and our neighbors as ourselves. Expel from our hearts every thought of hate, envy, greed, and vulgarity. Cause love, peace, joy, and gentleness to grow as lovely flowers and blossom in our lives. May thy reproofs correct us, thy warnings frighten us, and thy promises allure us on to the heavenly land. In the days of health and happiness, may we be humble. May the pains and adversities of life work in us those graces exemplified in the Christ-life. When shadows of death gather about us, O Lord, may we cling to thee. Be thou our guide across the river. Anchor us safely in the harbor of eternal repose. In Jesus' name. Amen.

c. Almighty God, the heavens declare thy majesty and thy

glory; and the firmament showeth thy handiwork. Day unto day uttereth speech, and night unto night showeth knowledge. Thy law is perfect, restoring the soul; thy testimony is sure, making wise the simple. Thy precepts are right, rejoicing the heart. The fear of thee is clean, enduring forever. More to be desired is thy word than gold, yea, than much fine gold; sweeter also than honey and the droppings of the honeycomb. By thy precious word thy servant is warned, and in keeping it there is great reward. Who can discern his errors? Clear thou me from hidden faults. Keep back thy servant also from presumptuous sins; let them not have dominion over me: Then shall I be upright, and I shall be clear from great transgression. Let the words of my mouth and the meditation of my heart be acceptable in thy sight, O Jehovah, my rock, and my redeemer. In the name of him who is the fulfillment of both law and prophecy. Amen.

d. O God of Peace, out of anxiety and anguish of heart, we cry unto thee. Bless our nation. Bless the nations of the earth. . . . We thank thee for our native land, with its green pastures, its fruit-bearing trees, its fertile fields, and its peace-loving people. We are grateful for our noble sons and precious daughters. May the grim figure of war never lift its cruel form in our midst to destroy, to cripple, and to kill. Grant that the bodies of our sons may never be torn by shot and shell, and that the forms of our daughters may never be ravaged by the beast of war. We thank thee for the gospel of peace and for the Prince of Peace concerning whom the angels sang on the break of day—

"Glory to God in the highest,
And on earth peace among men in whom he is well pleased."

May his blessed spirit dominate the thoughts and purposes of our rulers and of men everywhere. In his precious name. Amen.

e. Heavenly Father, Giver of all gifts, with grateful hearts we look unto thee. We thank thee:

For thyself—thy everlasting love, thy eternal faithfulness, thy unchanging nature;

For Jesus, heaven's love gift, and for the blessed hope he instills within us;

For the Spirit's coming, for his abode in our hearts, teaching, comforting, and guiding us through the gloom;

For the church, the Lamb's bride, for the fellowship it affords, for the salvation it enjoys, for the glory it anticipates;

For the home, for the memories the home awakens, for our children, for our parents, for all the precious ties of nature;

For the harvest, for the land of plenty, for deliverance from flood, famine, pestilence and war;

For life and life's varied experiences, bitter and sweet, knowing that, if we love thee supremely, all things will work out for our ultimate good and eternal glory.

Like the stars of the heavens, or as the sand which is upon the seashore, thy blessings are numberless. We thank thee for all. Grant that we may take them and use them wisely.

When life's fitful fever is over, and our work here is done, grant us an inheritance that is fairer than day. In the name of him for whom we thank thee most. Amen.

f. Our heavenly Father, thou art the Author and Maker of the home. We thank thee for the home—for the father, the mother, and the child who make it. We thank thee for the strength of the father who guides it, for the tenderness of the mother who adorns it, and for the cheerfulness of the child who blesses it.

Grant that the home may stand in its strength and loveliness even as thou hast ordained it, giving stability to the church, to the community, and to the nation.

May thy eternal truth be its guiding light, its firm foundation, its man of counsel, and its refuge. May the husband love and honor the wife, and the wife love, cherish, and obey the husband. May each be unto the child a safe example in manner of life, bringing it up in thy nurture and admonition.

In the name of him who honored and sanctified the home. Amen.

2. Each student in the class is asked to write out a prayer and bring it to class. After it is read aloud the instructor and the class will make suggestions.

CHAPTER VI

The Beginning Talk

SEVERAL SUGGESTIONS WILL be offered here to help in the preparation of beginning talks. Chapters to follow will make a more thorough approach to the subject of speechmaking, but now it is time to launch out on the first speech. There is absolutely no substitute for practice and experience, and all the principles of public speaking suggested in later pages will mean more to you after you have had some experience in standing before an audience. So, let us climb that first mountain.

THE BIOGRAPHICAL TALK

The easiest type of religious talk to make is the biographical talk. Not only is it the easiest for the speaker, but it is one of the most interesting to the audience and one of the most valuable. From every standpoint it is the logical place to begin, and here is how you do it:

1. **Choose some favorite Bible character as your subject.** Each of us has certain favorite Bible personalities. Maybe you have always especially enjoyed studying about David, or Joseph, or Daniel, or the apostle Paul. In any case choose a char-

acter for whom you have a special liking, and about whom you already know something. The more you already know, the easier this speaking assignment will be.

2. **Read the complete life story in the Bible.** If the subject of your talk is Joseph, you will turn to Genesis 37 and read that book to the end. Read deliberately and thoughtfully and, as you read, make a few notes on the most important facts of Joseph's life. When you have finished reading the Bible story you may want to turn to a good Bible dictionary for a brief summary of his life. In a good concordance you may find additional references to Joseph, scattered through the Bible. You might find still other material in some book of biographical studies of Bible characters, or in a sermon on your chosen personality. At the end of your reading you will have quite an array of facts about Joseph. Now, you are ready to organize your talk.

3. **Plan your talk.** The easiest and often the best approach is to tell the story as you have read it in the Bible—chronologically. Then you are not likely to forget what comes next. Tell first things first, then the things that happened next, until you have finished. Other arrangements may be more appropriate for some Bible characters. In dealing with King Saul, for example, the following might be of value: (a) his special abilities and promise of greatness, (b) his great blunders, and finally (c) his tragic downfall. For Samson, the outline might be: (a) his strength, (b) his weakness, and (c) his lessons for us.

4. **Point out some lessons or applications for your hearers.** After you have told the story of the person's life, there needs to be some suggestion of the relation his life has to your hearers. Imagine that one of your listeners was frank enough (or rude enough) to ask, "So what?" Tell him why you chose to speak about this character in terms of the valuable lessons his life teaches. The life of every Bible character is rich in applica-

tions to lives of men today. Look for these practical values and you will find them.

5. **Practice your talk aloud.** For confidence before an audience you need, above all, to know what you are going to say. Such knowledge comes through careful preparation and adequate practice. Memorize your plan, but don't memorize the entire talk. Just go over the talk aloud until you are sure of it. From five to ten times should be enough.

THE PARAGRAPH TALK

Another appropriate type of talk for beginning speakers is the paragraph talk. It develops as follows:

1. **Choose a paragraph of scripture especially appealing to you.** This might be Luke 5:1-11, about Jesus' stepping into Simon's boat on the Sea of Galilee, to preach a sermon to the multitude on the shore. At his request Simon then "put out into the deep" and let down the nets, making a miraculous catch of fish. He and James and John were so impressed that they left their boats and followed Jesus to become "fishers of men." There are hundreds of paragraphs in the Bible which are brimful of interest and also of value. They are just waiting for your use.

2. **Study the passage exhaustively.** Read the passage in your Bible over and over until you have the full meaning. Then, study it in some standard commentary. Talk with your friends and family about it. Live with it until you have really mastered it.

3. **Plan your talk.** Again, you need to have a plan. On a piece of paper, or preferably on a card, jot down the things you want to say, and arrange them in order. Your talk may be a verse-by-verse commentary on the paragraph, ending with special lessons or applications. Or you may read the paragraph aloud, lay the Bible aside, tell the story again in your own

words, and then point out its lessons. There are many ways, but each one benefits from being planned. Usually it is best to have the plan in writing.

4. **Practice your talk aloud.** As suggested above, go over and over your talk until you know just what you intend to say.

ACTIVITIES

1. Suggested subjects for biographical talks, with a point of contact in the scriptures:

a. Noah, Genesis 6.
b. Abram, Genesis 12.
c. Sarai, Genesis 12.
d. Isaac, Genesis 21.
e. Jacob, Genesis 25.
f. Joseph, Genesis 37.
g. Moses, Exodus 2.
h. Joshua, Joshua 1.
i. Samson, Judges 13:24–14:20.
j. Ruth, Ruth 1.
k. Samuel, I Samuel 1.
l. Saul, I Samuel 9.
m. David, I Samuel 16.
n. Solomon, II Samuel 12.
o. Elijah, I Kings 17.
p. Esther, Esther 1.
q. Daniel, Daniel 1.
r. Peter, Luke 5.
s. John, Matthew 10.
t. Paul, Acts 9.

2. Suggested passages for paragraph talks:

a. Genesis 22:1–19—Abraham Offers Isaac.
b. Exodus 20:1–17—The Ten Commandments.
c. Joshua 1:1–9—God's Charge to Joshua.
d. II Samuel 12:1–7—David's Sin.
e. Isaiah 53:1–12—Prophecy of the Messiah.
f. Matthew 5:1–12—The Beatitudes.
g. Matthew 6:5–13—Prayer.
h. Matthew 7:15–27—He That Doeth.
i. Matthew 13:1–9, 18–23—The Parable of the Sower.
j. Matthew 17:1–8—The Transfiguration.
k. Matthew 25:1–13—The Ten Virgins.
l. Luke 5:1–11—The Disciples Follow Jesus.

m. Luke 15:11-32—The Prodigal Son.
n. Luke 16:19-31—The Rich Man and Lazarus.
o. John 1:1-18—Christ Among Men.
p. John 4:1-26—True Worship.
q. Acts 5:1-11—Ananias and Sapphira.
r. I Corinthians 13:1-13—Love.
s. James 2:14-26—Faith Without Works.
t. James 3:1-12—The Tongue.

CHAPTER VII

Ten Commandments for
Effective Speaking

THE FOLLOWING CHAPTERS attempt to present comprehensively though briefly the principles of effective speaking, based on centuries of observation by thousands of thoughtful people. They contain nothing sensationally new or exciting, for their purpose is utter practicality. The innate common sense of alert students would discover most of the principles, in time; but the orderly classification of principles presented here will enable beginning speakers to master them more speedily and thoroughly. This is not to be taken as setting down anybody's strange, difficult, arbitrary whims, but is the congealed common sense of the ages on how to speak well.

It is appropriate to begin by setting forth the "Ten Commandments of Effective Speaking" so that the reader may have an over-all view. Later chapters will develop the separate principles in greater detail; but if you will memorize these "commandments" they will form a permanent foundation on which you can build speaking skill.

I. *Take Aim: Select a Goal Which You Can Achieve.*

To make possible an intelligent beginning at preparation for any speech, the speaker must set a goal for himself. Otherwise both the preparation and the speech will be "like a leaf dancing on a tree," constantly in movement, but getting nowhere. Many a speech lacks a proper goal, and its rambling, purposeless, fruitless nature is often painfully apparent to the audience and disappointing to the speaker. Before facing an audience a man needs to decide what he aims to accomplish, and of course it ought to be an aim within reach. Having chosen his goal, he should write it out in a purpose sentence—or proposition—and then direct all his efforts toward achieving it.

II. *Choose a Subject Which Fits You, the Occasion, and the Audience.*

Now the speaker is in a position to choose a subject. The number of possible subjects is determined primarily by three factors: (a) the speaker's own background of information or experience; (b) appropriateness or inappropriateness to the occasion; (c) the interests, training, and mood of the audience.

III. *Earn the Right to Speak by Adequate Work and Study.*

Before taking the time of other people a speaker should earn the right to speak by study and work that will enable him to give them something in return for their attention. A man who addresses one hundred people for half an hour has used up fifty hours of their collective time. A speech must contain a great deal of meat in order to be worthy of the time it takes; and that meat needs to be well prepared and ready to be assimilated.

IV. *Touch the Basic Human Motives—the Springs of Response.*

Man has certain basic desires, or drives, or urges. The speaker who achieves a high degree of success in influencing people has learned to direct his appeal to their God-given, basic human motives. It is comparatively ineffective to tell a man he ought to go to the Red Cross and give a pint of blood. Instead, point out that a pint of his blood will produce gamma globulin which will help to prevent "polio" from striking down his own or some other child.

V. *Make a Thorough Outline.*

Men are seldom moved by a careless, haphazard presentation of facts. They expect and appreciate some reasonable plan or system. In order to provide this a speaker usually must draft a careful outline of his material. His main headings stand out for special emphasis, and his subordinate points support them. Choosing and arranging the headings is of vital importance. The outline is to a speech what the skeleton is to the human body.

VI. *Begin and End the Speech in a Forceful Manner.*

The very beginning and the end are the places of greatest emphasis in any speech. If the speaker is to gain and hold the attention of his hearers, he must begin well, for the first few sentences often win or lose the battle. It may also be won or lost in the closing sentences. Often the entire speech is built toward a climax. An otherwise good speech can be ruined by a weak beginning or an ineffective close.

VII. *Be Concrete, Pictorial, and Vivid.*

Human beings think in terms of pictures. Henry Ward Beecher states, "He who would move men must either tell stories or paint pictures." It has been said, "One picture is worth a thousand words." It is the speaker's task to paint pictures with words, so that the hearers carry away concrete and vivid impressions rather than vague concepts or generalities.

VIII. *Keep Moving Toward Your Goal.*

Hundreds of interesting side roads beckon to the traveler when he sets out on a journey, but he must ignore them in order to reach his destination. So, in speaking, every subject that one might choose has many related side areas that must be ignored. Before any fact, quotation, illustration, or other piece of material is introduced into a speech it must face the exacting question: "Does it aid in achieving the goal?"

IX. *Practice Aloud.*

However wonderfully composed a speech may be, it is all for nothing if the speaker forgets it or garbles it in delivery. Repeated oral practice is the best precaution. Go over and over the outline until the plan is vivid in your mind, and until words to put flesh and blood on the skeleton come easily.

X. *Be Enthusiastic, Genial, and Conversational When You Speak.*

If the proof of the pudding is in the eating, the test of a speech is in the delivery. All that goes before may be in vain unless it is effectively delivered. In our age the simple, direct, conversational style is best. Say what you have to say in animated, enthusiastic fashion, and as simply and directly as you can. A speaker who likes people and lets them know it will be liked in return.

As was said at the beginning of the chapter, these "Ten Commandments" form a foundation of good speaking. Memorize them, and begin to put them into practice. They will be discussed in detail in the pages to come.

TEN COMMANDMENTS FOR EFFECTIVE SPEAKING

I. Take aim: Select a goal which you can achieve.

II. Choose a subject which fits you, the occasion, and the audience.

III. Earn the right to speak by adequate work and study.

IV. Touch the basic human motives—the springs of response.

V. Make a thorough outline.

VI. Begin and end the speech in a forceful manner.

VII. Be concrete, pictorial, and vivid.

VIII. Keep moving toward your goal.

IX. Practice aloud.

X. Be enthusiastic, genial, and conversational when you speak.

ARE YOU DISCOURAGED YET?

Several weeks ago when our efforts to become better speakers for the Lord began, your enthusiasm was high, and your determination was strong. How is it now? Do you need to stop and think again about how important this work is? Your success will depend largely on the intensity of your desire to become an effective speaker. Ponder carefully the following quotations:

I never allow myself to become discouraged under any circumstances. . . . The three great essentials to achieve anything worth while are, first, hard work; second, stick-to-itiveness; third, common sense.   —THOMAS A. EDISON

> If you think you are beaten, you are.
> If you think you dare not, you don't.
> If you'd like to win, but think you can't,
> It's almost a cinch you won't.
> Life's battles don't always go
> To the stronger or faster man;
> But soon or late the man who wins
> Is the one who thinks he can.
>   —ANONYMOUS

If you are resolutely determined to make a lawyer of yourself, the thing is more than half done already. . . . Always bear in mind that your own resolution to succeed is more important than any other one thing.   —ABRAHAM LINCOLN

They can conquer who believe they can. . . . He has not learned the first lesson of life who does not every day surmount a fear.
—RALPH WALDO EMERSON

Never take counsel of your fears.
—MOTTO OF ANDREW JACKSON

But Jesus said unto him, No man, having put his hand to the plow, and looking back, is fit for the kingdom of God.   —LUKE 9:62

ACTIVITIES

1. Each member of the class should be prepared to give the "Ten Commandments" listed here from memory. Memorize the sentences exactly as they are—word for word.

2. Be prepared to stand before the class and explain each of these commandments.

CHAPTER VIII

Taking Aim

THERE IS A story of an old janitor employed by a large and fashionable church. In addition to his regular duties he took part in the preparations for occasional church dinners, setting up the tables and folding chairs and helping with the dishes and the silver. Often he would be working feverishly after the crowd had begun to gather, and on one such occasion he was seen starting down an aisle with a stack of dishes. When it closed so that he could not get through he reversed his field and tried another aisle. It too became clogged, and he had to turn another way. One of the men of the church stepped over and asked, "Uncle, how do you ever manage to get your work done in all this hustle and bustle?" The old man replied, "Well, boss, I jest shifts my mind into nootral and goes where I'se pushed."

The story has striking parallels in many talks and sermons. They seem not to aim at anything, but simply to go willy-nilly wherever the current pushes them. A major difference between a great speech and one of little consequence is that the great speech has a real goal and never forgets its destination. There is no more important principle in speaking than having a purpose; and no single fault produces more failures than lack of aim.

Henry Ward Beecher, addressing the young men at Yale University, told this story of his boyhood:

> I used to go out hunting by myself, and I had great success in firing off my gun; and the game enjoyed it as much as I did, for I never hit them or hurt them. I fired off my gun as I see hundreds of men firing off their sermons. I loaded it, and bang!—there was a smoke, a report, but nothing fell; and so it was again and again. I recollect one day in the fields my father pointed out a little red squirrel, and said to me, "Henry, would you like to shoot him?" I trembled all over, but I said, "Yes." He got down on his knee, put the gun across a rail, and said, "Henry, keep perfectly cool, perfectly cool; take aim." And I did, and I fired, and over went the squirrel, and he didn't run away either. That was the first thing I ever hit; and I felt an inch taller, as a boy that had killed a squirrel, and knew how to aim a gun.[1]

In the several pages of the published book following this illustration, Beecher told of his first successful sermon. Because of discouraging results during his first two years as a preacher, he had made a careful study of the methods of the apostles. Concluding that their success resulted from a complete understanding of their hearers, and from a careful adaptation of their sermons to them, he resolved to imitate their methods, and carefully planned a sermon to fit his own audience. There were seventeen responses. He had learned how to take aim.

William M. Taylor also emphasized the importance of aiming at something:

> Every sermon should have a distinct object in view. One must preach, not because . . . he has to occupy the time somehow, but

---

[1]Beecher, *Yale Lectures on Preaching,* Vol. I, p. 10.

rather because there is something pressing upon his mind and heart which he feels impelled to proclaim. . . .

Ever, therefore, as you sit down to prepare your discourse, let your question be, "What is my purpose in this sermon?" and do not move a step until you have shaped out before your mind a definite answer to that inquiry.[2]

The famous Irish political orator Daniel O'Connell once said, "The man who aims at nothing is sure to hit it." The wise public speaker might well say of his speech what the apostle Paul said of his life: "But one thing I do, forgetting the things which are behind, and stretching forward to the things which are before, I press on toward the goal."[3]

FOUR GENERAL GOALS OF SPEAKING

There are basically four types of response which a speaker may wish to obtain from his audience. In planning his speech he should aim at one or more of these.

1. **To interest.** In this type of speech the purpose is to keep the audience listening. Either through humor or through more serious material it endeavors to make the audience wish to hear more. All purely entertaining speeches are of this type. Travelogues and descriptions of strange, new inventions might also fall within this area. This type of goal could never be appropriate for religious speaking, because the purpose of the religious speaker is always higher than mere entertainment. True, he might sometimes use humor or the entertaining quality as a subordinate means of achieving a higher purpose. It is fine for audiences to enjoy a religious talk or a sermon; but enjoyment should not be its chief aim.

2. **To inform.** The purpose of informative speaking is to dis-

[2]Taylor, *The Ministry of the Word*, pp. 110–11.
[3]Philippians 3:13–14.

seminate facts, to create understanding, so that the audience will end by knowing more than before and understanding the new facts so clearly and so well that they will be remembered. Obviously, much religious speaking has this goal.

3. **To stimulate.** Speaking which aims to stimulate brings into new prominence something that has been believed or accepted in times past. This type is needed, because even strong convictions fade unless revived—often the sparks of yesterday's fire will die unless they are fanned into a new flame. Much religious speaking is designed to revitalize old desires, intentions, or ideals.

4. **To convince.** Here the purpose is to change the thinking of persons whose convictions differ with those of the speaker. Logical reasoning and judicious emotional appeal, based on facts, figures, and examples, characterize such speeches. Probably the most difficult of all, the convincing speech also pays the greatest dividends. All other types of speaking are used as support for this crowning type.

In the light of this discussion it should be clear that good speakers study the speech situation in which they are to participate—carefully analyzing the occasion, the audience, and the speaker's relationship to each—and then decide on the response which they wish to win from the audience. This goal should be within the limits of possibility. For example, it is of little value to urge a group of elementary school children to vote for Senator So-and-so. Choose a goal you can achieve. The success of the speech, then, is measured in terms of the degree to which the goal is achieved. The only valid criterion by which to measure is, "Did the speaker do what he set out to do?"

CHOOSING THE SUBJECT

After settling on his purpose the speaker is ready to select subject. The desired response will often almost automati-

cally indicate the topic, and sometimes the two are so inter-
woven that they are chosen almost simultaneously. In making
certain that the subject is appropriate for the occasion the
speaker has to consider several important factors: the audience; the occasion; and himself.

THE AUDIENCE

Audiences differ in scores of ways, and it is imperative that
the speaker have a clear concept of his audience before choosing his topic and beginning his preparation. The following factors are often included in an audience analysis chart:

1. Size of the audience.
2. Sex of its members.
3. Ages represented.
4. Educational backgrounds represented.
5. Occupations represented.
6. Organizations—religious, social, and professional—
represented.
7. Chief interests and motives present.
8. Beliefs, attitudes, and convictions present.
9. Existing knowledge of the subject.
10. Attitude of the audience toward the speaker.

Taking these factors into consideration, the speaker can
choose a subject adapted to the group to which he is to speak
and thus have a running start toward achieving the response
desired.

THE OCCASION

The occasion often suggests an appropriate subject. The
various seasons of the year—the New Year with its new begin-
nings, the spring with its resurgence of life, the various days of
special national significance, the days of religious significance,
the period of Thanksgiving—all suggest themes that are appropriate. A special speech principle is involved here. Good

speakers always try to begin speaking "where the people are." In other words, try to connect what you say to the things that the audience has been thinking about. This beginning on *common ground* gets the speech off to a good start.

The fact that occasions differ and therefore call for very different treatments should always be borne in mind. A funeral is to be approached in a vastly different way from a wedding, or from a regular religious service. The mood of the audience is vital. The speaker must adapt his speaking to the mood of the hearers. In addition, he should know something about the purpose for which the audience has come together, the plan of the meeting or service, and the physical setting. In all these, danger lurks unless he knows about them and adapts his speech to them.

THE SPEAKER

The speaker should always choose a subject about which he already has background knowledge, and in which he has a deep interest. Otherwise his treatment is likely to be bookish. Illustrations or experiences drawn from real life are especially valuable. Judiciously presented, these add interest and force to a speech. One young man working at Lockheed Aircraft Corporation during World War II chose to speak on "Plane Christianity" and drew a number of parallels between flying and Christianity. He thus made a contribution other speakers could not make.

The age and the experience of the speaker are also factors to be considered. A young man can hardly be expected to deal satisfyingly with the more profound subjects of the Bible, such as "The Reason for Suffering," "The Unpardonable Sin," or "The Prophecies of Revelation." An older man may be limited by age and physical weakness. Experience in speaking should also receive full consideration, for in no other way can a speaker prepare himself fully to handle difficult situations. His own deep convictions and special interests will often suggest subjects which are ideally suited to his use.

SUMMARY

Alan Monroe's excellent textbook *Principles and Types of Speech* gives the following suggestions for the selection of a subject. They will serve as a comprehensive summary of what has been said:

"Select a subject about which you already know something and can find out more.

"Select a subject that is interesting to you.

"Select a subject that will interest your audience:

"a. Because it vitally concerns their affairs.

"b. Because it concerns the solution of a definite problem.

"c. Because it is new or timely.

"d. Because there is a conflict of opinion on it.

"Select a subject that is not above or below the intellectual capacity of the audience.

"Select a subject that you can discuss adequately in the time you have at your disposal."[4]

ACTIVITIES

1. Before coming to class let each member select three situations in which he might some time be called to speak. For each he should select an appropriate speech purpose and subject.

2. In the class period let each person make a brief speech explaining one or more of these situations and explaining and defending his choice of purpose and subject.

---

[4]From *Principles and Types of Speech* by Alan H. Monroe. Copyright, 1949, by Scott, Foresman and Company, and reprinted with their permission. Pp. 164–65.

CHAPTER IX

Delivery

THE DELIVERY OF a speech has two aspects—what people see, and what people hear. Here we are concerned with the visible aspects of delivery; the chapter following will be concerned with the audible aspects. Francis Bacon told of a question once asked of Demosthenes: "What is the chief part of an orator?" He answered, "Action." "What next?" "Action." "What next again?" "Action." Surely this is overstatement; but it is true that what an audience sees is important. First of all, a speaker should be properly groomed before he stands before his audience: he should be clean and neatly dressed; his hair should be combed; and his clothes should be in keeping with the style of the day but not showy or distracting.

CONVERSATIONAL STYLE

"When the delivery is really good," said Archbishop Whately, "the hearers never think about it, but are exclusively occupied with the sense it conveys, and the feelings it excites." It would be difficult to find a better way to introduce the idea of a conversational speaking style. Particularly in our day, audiences are attracted by a simple, straightforward, enthusiastic communication of ideas—the kind of thing that each of us does every day. Incidentally, this makes public speaking so much easier—if some high-flown, elaborate style were required, many of us would never make the grade. Instead, the best of all speaking is the very kind we have been doing daily for years.

James A. Winans, noted modern-day rhetorician, puts it graphically:

> Here comes a man who has seen a great race, or has been in a battle, or perhaps is excited about his new invention, or on fire with enthusiasm for a cause. He begins to talk with a friend on the street. Others join them, five, ten, twenty, a hundred. Interest grows. He lifts his voice that all may hear; but the crowd wishes to hear and see the speaker better. "Get up on this truck!" they cry; and he mounts the truck and goes on with his story or his plea.
>
> A private conversation has become a public speech; but under the circumstances imagined it is thought of only as a conversation, an enlarged conversation. It does not seem abnormal, but quite the natural thing.
>
> When does the converser become a speech-maker? When ten persons gather? Fifty? Or is it when he gets on the truck? There is, of course, no point at which we can say the change has taken place. There is no change in the nature or the spirit of the act; it is essentially the same throughout, a conversation adapted as the speaker proceeds to the growing number of hearers. . . . He is conversing with an audience.[1]

Conversational speaking is merely enlarged conversation, somewhat louder, somewhat better organized, and somewhat more formal. But remember above all else to keep it conversational. The enthusiasm, the spontaneity, and the directness are essential to good speaking.

---

[1] James A. Winans, *Speech-Making,* pp. 11–12. Used by permission of Appleton-Century-Crofts, Inc.

ENTHUSIASM

"Nothing great," said Emerson, "was ever achieved without enthusiasm." In the delivery of a speech there is no quality more important than earnestness. As Phillips Brooks, one of the Yale lecturers on preaching, said, "Nothing but fire kindles fire."[2] Along this line William Jennings Bryan said:

Eloquence may be defined as the speech of one who knows what he is talking about, and means what he says—it is thought on fire. . . . Knowledge is of little use to the speaker without earnestness. Persuasiveness is from heart to heart, not from mind to mind. . . . Nearly two thousand years ago, one of the Latin poets expressed this thought when he said: "If you would draw tears from others' eyes, yourself the signs of grief must show."

Time after time I have heard beginning speakers make dull, unimpressive speeches. They were dull not because the material was uninteresting, but because there was no life or enthusiasm in the delivery. At times I have challenged facts, not because I really doubted their authenticity, but because I wanted to hear the speaker come alive in their defense and put all that he had into it. "If I wish to compose or write or pray or preach well," said Martin Luther, "I must be angry. Then all the blood in my veins is stirred, and my understanding is sharpened."

The James-Lange theory of the emotions is especially valuable for public speakers. It holds that physical action can arouse or stimulate the emotions. Most people think that only the opposite is true—that aroused emotions lead to physical action. Actually, both are true. If you feel timid and fearful and unenthusiastic before an audience, force yourself to be enthusiastic, to move about the platform, to use gestures. Then,

---

[2]Brooks, *Lectures on Preaching*, p. 38.

before you know it, you will begin to feel enthusiastic. Try it and see.

When our Puritan forefathers were in their prime the preachers often would preach two hours or more at a time. Because human flesh was weak at best, it was necessary for the sexton to stand at the back of the church with a long pole. At one end of it was a round knob with which he prodded the men who dozed, and at the other end was a feather with which he tickled the ladies who nodded. For our day it is recommended that, when listeners become sleepy, someone take the long pole, walk forward, and *prod the preacher.* When people become uninterested or sleepy, it is usually the speaker's fault. Be enthusiastic. "I like the man," said John G. Shedd, president of Marshall Field and Company, "who bubbles over with enthusiasm. Better to be a geyser than a mud puddle."

POSTURE AND MOVEMENT

When walking to the platform, walk so as to create confidence; walk as one who knows where he is going, and why he is going there. Neither hurry nor lag, but take your position as one who has a right to be there. After you have reached your speaking position, pause a moment to turn and look the audience squarely in the eye and see that all are looking directly at you. Then begin to speak.

The basic elements of good posture are dignity, balance, poise, stability, and directness. Stand comfortably erect—*stand tall.* Do not stand stiffly erect as in the military posture: this is artificial and would make natural, easy, conversational speech almost impossible. Place both feet solidly on the floor, but not so as to appear "planted" and incapable of movement. Nearly always, one foot will be slightly ahead of the other, with the toes pointing slightly outward, as in walking. The chest should be held up; hips, back.

The eyes should look directly into the faces of the audience.
Nothing is more important in the study of delivery than establishing eye-contact with your hearers. Do not look above their heads; do not look down at the floor; look at them. Have no regular pattern of movement, but cover the entire group from time to time while speaking. Think of your line of vision as a kind of invisible bridge over which your ideas flow into the minds of your listeners. Look at one person for several moments, letting the thoughts flow in; then move on to someone else, then to a third, and so on until you have covered the entire audience. Surprisingly, as long as you are really looking at someone—eye to eye—everyone else will feel that you are looking at him, too.

"What shall I do with my hands?" is often asked. Let them hang easily at the sides. Do not try to hide them, for they are not nearly so big or so awkward as you imagine. Do not try to hide them in pockets or behind you. Use the several hand positions, but no one of them overmuch. Let the arms bend at the elbows, thus putting the hands—one or both—in front of the body. Do not clasp the hands in front of the body, however, for this is a relatively weak position. Occasionally, they may go behind you—but get them back to home base, hanging loosely at the sides, more often than anywhere else.

Platform movement should avoid the extreme of standing stock-still all the time, or of moving about like a caged lion. Ordinarily, movements should be made forward and backward rather than from side to side. Forward movement is for emphasis; backward movement is for transition. Side-to-side movement may possibly serve to show transitions of thought, but often degenerates into meaningless, nervous movement.

In all your platform behavior, let your attitude be one of making friends. Friendliness begets friendliness, but the initiative must be yours. Just as in a mirror, you usually get back about what you send. Let your facial expression be pleasant always. "Smile, and the world smiles with you," is good advice for the speaker, though of course the smile should not be a smirk and should not be overdone.

GESTURES

A gesture is a movement of any part of the body—head, shoulders, arms, hands—to convey some thought or feeling or to enforce the oral expression of a thought or feeling. Sometimes speakers fear that gestures may appear awkward or ungainly. Actually no speaker can afford to speak without this important means of supporting his oral presentation. Herbert Spencer pointed out the value of gestures:

To say "Leave the room" is less expressive than to point to the door. Placing the finger on the lips is more forcible than whispering "Do not speak." A beck of the hand is better than "Come here." No phrase can convey the idea of surprise so vividly as opening the eyes and raising the eyebrows. A shrug of the shoulders would lose much by translation into words.

Gestures help communicate ideas, they help hold attention, and they also increase the speaker's confidence. The best advice is to become familiar with the various types of gestures, practice them in privacy, and then use them when inner impulses dictate. Nothing is worse than artificial gestures imposed upon a speech from outside. The gestures must come from within the speaker. After he has studied the various kinds and has practiced them for a while, they will come to his aid spontaneously when he feels something deeply and wants to get it across to an audience.

There are basically two types of gestures: *descriptive* and *conventionalized.*

1. **Descriptive gestures** actually endeavor to describe the object, movement, or idea being discussed. The action is imita-

tive. The size, shape, or weight of an object is easily indicated. The movement of an object can also be conveyed without difficulty. Descriptive gestures are most common and are very helpful.

2. **Conventionalized gestures:** Through the centuries certain movements have come to have a standardized, universal meaning. Nodding the head up and down has come to mean Yes, while head movement from side to side means No. The same kind of thing has taken place with certain hand movements. These are the standardized, conventionalized gestures. They are understood anywhere and fit any language. Some of the most widely used are:

a. *Open hand, palm up* signifies friendship, exchange of ideas, giving and receiving.

b. *Pointing, index finger* (and others) indicates direction and calls attention to objects; gives emphasis.

c. *Open hand, palm facing audience* means rejection or negation.

d. *Open hand, palm downward* suggests caution.

e. *Open hand, moved from side to side, palm held vertically,* gives the idea of dividing or separating into sections.

f. *Clenched fist* indicates strong feeling or great emphasis. These are the six basic, conventionalized gestures, but they can be, and often are, modified to suit the personality of the speaker and the requirements of the occasion. Practice each in connection with one of the passages included at the end of the chapter until you feel relative ease and freedom in its use. Only practice will make the use smooth and effective.

The speaker must let the entire body enter into the gestures as one well coordinated unit. Gestures of the arms or hands, unsustained by the head and the torso, are mechanical and awkward. Let the body function as a unit. In making gestures the speaker must always look at the audience and never at the gestures.

Each gesture has three phases: the approach, the stroke, and the return. In the approach the arms move into the position from which the gesture is to be made; in the return the arms move back to their normal position. Both movements should be made slowly so as not to draw the attention of the audience. The gesture itself is the stroke—the part the audience sees. It should be so timed that the stroke falls exactly upon the word or phrase which the speaker wishes to emphasize. Spontaneity and naturalness are the chief ends sought in good gesturing.

ACTIVITIES

1. Stand in front of a full-length mirror and practice making each of the conventionalized gestures named above until you can make it easily and naturally.

2. Read the following selections aloud, using the number and kind of gestures which the thought seems to require:

a. And he spake to them many things in parables, saying, Behold, the sower went forth to sow; and as he sowed, some seeds fell by the way side, and the birds came and devoured them: and others fell upon the rocky places, where they had not much earth: and straightway they sprang up, because they had no deepness of earth: and when the sun was risen, they were scorched; and because they had no root, they withered away. And others fell upon the thorns; and the thorns grew up and choked them: and others fell upon the good ground, and yielded fruit, some a hundred-fold, some sixty, some thirty. He that hath ears, let him hear. —MATTHEW 13:3–9

b. Fourscore and seven years ago our fathers brought forth on this continent, a new nation, conceived in liberty, and dedicated to the proposition that all men are created equal.

Now we are engaged in a great civil war, testing whether that nation, or any nation so conceived and so dedicated, can long endure. We are met on a great battlefield of that war. We have come to dedicate a portion of that field, as a final resting place for those who here gave their lives that that nation might live. It is altogether fitting and proper that we should do this.

But, in a larger sense, we cannot dedicate—we cannot consecrate—we cannot hallow—this ground. The brave men, living and dead, who struggled here have consecrated it, far above our poor power to add or detract. The world will little note, nor long remember what we say here, but it can never forget what they did here. It is for us the living, rather, to be dedicated here to the unfinished work which they who fought here have thus far so nobly advanced. It is rather for us to be here dedicated to the great task remaining before us—that from these honored dead we take increased devotion to that cause for which they gave the last full measure of devotion—that we here highly resolve that these dead shall not have died in vain—that this nation, under God, shall have a new birth of freedom—and that government of the people, by the people, for the people, shall not perish from the earth. —ABRAHAM LINCOLN

c. I am aware, that many object to the severity of my language; but is there not cause for severity? I *will be* as harsh as truth, and as uncompromising as justice. On this subject I do not wish to think, or speak, or write, with moderation. No! no! Tell a man whose house is on fire, to give a moderate alarm; tell him to moderately rescue his wife from the hands of the ravisher; tell the mother gradually to extricate her babe from the fire into which it has fallen:—but urge me not to use moderation in a cause like the present. I am in earnest—I will not equivocate— I will not excuse—I will not retreat a single inch—AND I will BE HEARD. The apathy of the people is enough to make every statue leap from its pedestal, and to hasten the resurrection of the dead. —WILLIAM LLOYD GARRISON

d. Nor must a young man compare himself with others or measure his success by theirs. It makes no difference how other men succeed. Their success is theirs; not yours. It matters nothing to me that Edison can invent the electric light and I can't; that Kipling can write a "Recessional" and I can't; that you can plead the law and I can't. You can do one thing; I try to do another. But success is for both of us just so far as we do well what we can do. Every man is himself, and it is in proportion as he gets out of himself the power there is within him that he succeeds—succeeds in doing the thing he is best fitted to do.

—EDWARD WILLIAM BOK

3. Prepare one of these passages for presentation before the class. You may give it from memory or read from the book. In either case use gestures freely; overdo during practice.

CHAPTER X

Improving the Voice

ALTHOUGH EACH OF us is born with a physical mechanism ideally suited for producing speech, most of us learn to talk without knowing much about the mechanism itself. Even after using it for years we are often still quite unaware of the various parts of the speech mechanism and the contribution each makes. This lack of knowledge presents no great problem, for men often learn to use instruments which they do not understand. Take the automobile, for example. It is possible to be a good driver without knowing how to dismantle a motor. Similarly many good speakers know nothing at all about the physical aspects of speech production. However, in order to improve the performance of the instrument we are using—car, typewriter, speech mechanism, or any other—we must learn something about the mechanism and how it works.

That is the procedure we shall adopt now.

We have been speaking for many years, and have learned some careless, inefficient habits. Voice faults have crept into our daily usage, so that we have come to speak perhaps with marked nasality, or with a noticeable huskiness, or without proper clarity and distinctness. Or we may have developed one of the other common faults. One who is learning to speak for the Lord needs to overcome any such fault and develop a full, resonant, attractive voice, for the voice plays a major part in the effectiveness of speech. A poor voice is a constant handicap and may defeat any other speaking virtue that may be acquired. A good voice is almost half the battle in good speaking. The first step is to learn how the voice is produced.

The speech mechanism is a marvelously constructed instrument, and is evidence of the fact that we are "fearfully and wonderfully made." For the purpose of study, it can be divided into four parts:

1. **The motor**. The initial source of all speech power resides in what is generally called the motor—consisting of the lungs, the bronchial tubes, the bony structure of the chest, and the muscles that surround the lungs. This entire mechanism is essentially a pump for compressing air, which in turn is used to set the speech process in motion. The process begins when the muscles which control the ribs—a bony thoracic cage, which surrounds and protects the lungs—raise them upward and outward and thus give the lungs room to expand. At the same time the diaphragm muscle and others immediately below the lungs are pulled down, giving them room to expand downward also. A vacuum is formed, and air from outside the body rushes into the lungs. This is called inhalation. Next, the muscles controlling the ribs begin to contract, pulling them inward and downward around the lungs. At the same time the diaphragm muscle moves upward, crowding the lungs from the bottom. The only possible result is for the lungs to become smaller, by pushing the air out through the throat. This is called exhalation. The whole process resembles the working of a bellows. The escaping air is the motive power for speech.

2. **The vibrator.** The air from the lungs escapes through the

trachea into the larynx, or voice box, or Adam's apple, where the vocal cords are. These "vocal lips," which in normal quiet breathing lie relaxed at the sides of the air passage, can be brought close together with the result that the air passing through vibrates, producing sound for speech.

3. **The resonators.** The sound produced by the vocal folds or lips is a rather quiet, timid buzzing that needs to be built up and made forceful. This is the work of the resonators: the air chambers of the throat, nasal cavities, sinuses, and mouth, helped by the bony structure of the head. The resonators amplify the sound, making it louder. They also affect its quality, making it rich and mellow or thin and pinched.

4. **The articulators.** After the sound has been produced and enlarged it has to be divided into syllables and words by the articulators—tongue, lips, teeth, palate, jaw, and so on—through a careful coordination that modifies the size and shape of the resonating cavities, incidentally helping in the process of resonation.

SUGGESTIONS FOR GOOD SPEAKING

Now it is possible to point out several requirements for a good speaking voice. These are essentially suggestions for the use of the speech mechanism just explained.

1. **Proper control of breathing** is the important thing, not the amount of air that can be taken into the lungs. Inhalation for speech is deeper and more rapid than for normal breathing. Exhalation must be more forceful and better controlled than in normal breathing. There are three levels of breathing —upper chest, middle chest, and abdominal—and all are to be used by the speaker. However, the main control of breathing should be in the diaphragm muscle, far removed from the throat where muscular tension is harmful to speech tones. At

the end of the chapter are several excellent exercises to develop good breathing.

2. **Relaxation of the throat and neck.** Pleasing voice quality can result only when the throat and neck are relaxed. Muscular tension here brings strain and soreness, and is heard by the audience in hard, inflexible tones. Improper breath control often causes strain in the neck and throat and it is for this reason that the main control of breathing should be in the muscles of the abdomen.

3. **Flexible and energetic use of the articulators.** In order to achieve clear, distinct speech the articulators must be active. One of the dominant American speech faults is lip-laziness. Agility of the tongue, flexibility of the lips, and movability of the jaw are essential for the avoidance of mumbling and indistinct sound. Several exercises to develop these qualities are included at the end of the chapter.

COMMON VOICE FAULTS

Speech instruction comes so late to the average person that it is small wonder that most of us have various "minor speech defects." Because such defects have the strength of habit, we cannot expect to change them overnight; but most of them can be overcome by faithful practice. The common faults are explained below, with suggestions for overcoming them.

1. **Nasality.** The whining quality of voice which we call nasality is the nasalizing of non-nasal sounds. Only three sounds in our language are primarily nasal: *m, n,* and *ng.* When other sounds are allowed to have much nasal resonance the fault of nasality results. On the other hand, it is possible to give the three sounds too little nasal resonance. Then the result is a "denasal" quality.

As in most speech faults, the cause is probably a careless

production of speech throughout the entire process. Begin treatment by making certain that your breathing is adequate in amount and is properly controlled. Be sure the throat is relaxed. Then, make sure that the modifiers or articulators function energetically. Check to be sure the mouth is open wide enough, the lips and tongue are alert and active, and the lower jaw is flexible, and then concentrate upon the soft palate.

The soft palate, or uvula, which is the gatekeeper between the mouth and nose, is the organ of primary concern in nasality. If it is sluggish and inactive, nasality is inevitable. To make sure that it functions adequately, practice the following:

a. Hung-ah-ung, hung-ah-ung, hung-ah-ung, hung-ah-ung, hung-ah-ung. Hung-ah-ung, hung-ah-ung, hung-ah-ung, hung-ah-ung, hung-ah-ung. Hung-ah-ung, hung-ah-ung, hung-ah-ung, hung-ah-ung, hung-ah-ung.

b. Spend several minutes each day in humming. Allow the sound to build up in volume until you can feel the vibrations in the cheeks and other muscles of the face.

c. Devote several minutes each day to imitating the non-nasal voice quality of the better radio speakers. Listen to a phrase or sentence, then see if you can say it as pleasingly as the radio announcer. Imitate the quality of tone.

2. **Thinness** of voice is caused by a lack of force or carrying power. The voice is weak and flabby and can hardly be heard at the back of a room of even moderate size. The fault is primarily in the breathing mechanism.

Deeper breathing and a greater dependence upon abdominal breathing should help. In addition, it may be well to lower the pitch. Practice the breathing exercises at the end of the chapter until good strong breath support for the tones is achieved. At the same time work on the exercises for improving resonance.

3. **Harshness** is a rather hard, strident, metallic quality that results from constriction by muscles that are too tight or tense. It often accompanies hypertension or a high degree of nervousness. It also often results from an effort to speak loudly in the wrong way—by "pinching the throat" and thus forcing the constrictor muscles to become taut rather than by furnishing more breath from the abdomen.

The remedy is to learn to relax the neck and throat and to furnish the power for speaking from the diaphragm. Practice the exercises for relaxation and for correct breathing and good resonance at the end of the chapter.

4. **Hoarseness or huskiness** may have its explanation in infected sinuses, or in growths or nodules on the vocal cords resulting from much overloud speaking. In such cases the trouble is physical, and a physician should be consulted. More often, however, this quality of voice results from an attempt to lower the pitch below the natural range. Sometimes this is unconscious, but in other cases it is conscious because the speaker desires a deeper, richer voice than his normal one. The fault is known as "speaker's chronic sore throat."

The remedy is to relax the throat and raise the pitch to its normal level. Practice the relaxation exercises at the end of the chapter along with the exercises to develop proper breathing and resonation. The proper pitch for any voice may be determined by going to the piano and (1) finding the highest note that can be comfortably reached; (2) finding the lowest note that can be comfortably reached; and then (3) coming up the pitch scale one-third of the distance from the low note to the high note. This note is your *optimum pitch*—your ideal home base—and although your pitch will fluctuate well above and below it as your thought demands, this note should be approximately the average of all the fluctuations up and down.

5. **Breathiness** is a fuzzy quality of voice that suggests a part-whisper, which in a sense it is. It results from a failure to bring the edges of the vocal cords completely together in the production of voice, so that some of the air escapes unvoiced. The speaker never seems to have enough breath, for he wastes a large portion of what he has.

The best way to overcome the fault is through the practice of the "glottal catch." Allow a stream of unvocalized air to flow from the lungs (just breathe out) and then suddenly stop the flow of air by bringing the vocal cords together in the throat. You will hear a click, and the air will stop coming out. Be sure the stoppage is in the larynx, not just in the back of the mouth. Practice this over and over until the vocal cords become more active.

ACTIVITIES

1. For relaxation:

a. Close the eyes. Let the lower jaw drop; let it hang a dead weight from the axis. Let the tongue loll out of the mouth. Feel the muscles of the eyelids and eyeballs calm, quiet, and sleepy. Feel the muscles of the cheeks and lips flabby. Feel the muscles around the nose and forehead flabby. Feel the inside of the throat and nose relaxed so that air can pass in and out unobstructed.

b. With the muscles in this relaxed condition, allow the head to roll around slowly, making a complete rotation in each direction; repeat two or three times.

c. Yawn several times with all muscles completely relaxed.

d. Bend forward at the hips until the torso is parallel to the floor, with arms hanging inert. Then, jiggle the shoulders up and down (one up, the other down alternately) with arms and hands flopping inertly below.

2. For breathing:

a. Lie down in your own room, and let the body relax. Breathe naturally and deeply. With one hand on the abdomen and one on the chest, determine where the breathing activity centers. Usually, when the body is completely relaxed the breathing will be centered near the abdomen.

b. Stand comfortably erect with your back against a solid wall. Place a hand on abdomen. Inhale slowly and deeply. The hand should be pushed outward by correct breathing. Exhale slowly and fully. The hand should move inward. This is a test of correct breathing.

c. Inhale slowly, using the diaphragm muscle, until your lungs are full. Hold the air in the lungs by controlling the muscles around them. Leave the mouth and throat completely open. See how long you can hold your breath thus—from below.

d. Practice panting like a dog. Notice that the quick, short action in inhalation and exhalation is controlled by the diaphragm muscle.

e. Inhale slowly and fully. Count slowly: 1, 2, 3, etc., and see how far you can go while exhaling one breath. Repeat this exercise until you can count to fifty or beyond before the breath is exhausted.

3. For resonance: With relaxed throat, and with full, comfortable breath supply, read the following passages in a full, round, pleasant tone:

> a. Alone, alone, all, all alone,
> Alone on a wide, wide sea!
> And never a saint took pity on
> My soul in agony.

> —COLERIDGE

b. God of our fathers, known of old,
    Lord of our far-flung battle-line,
    Beneath whose awful Hand we hold
      Dominion over palm and pine—
Lord God of Hosts, be with us yet,
Lest we forget—lest we forget!
          —KIPLING

c. Roll on, thou deep and dark blue Ocean, roll!—BYRON

d. The curfew tolls the knell of parting day,
    The lowing herd winds slowly o'er the lea,
    The plowman homeward plods his weary way,
    And leaves the world to darkness and to me.
          —GRAY

e. Break, break, break,
    On thy cold gray stones, O Sea!
  And I would that my tongue could utter
    The thoughts that arise in me.
          —TENNYSON

f. Practice humming as a means of developing full resonance.

4. For the articulators:

a. Move the lips rapidly, or bite them to make the blood flow freely through them. Take extreme positions with them, moving quickly from a wide smile to a whistle position.

b. Practice the following rapidly and very lightly:

me-mo-mo-me, mo-me-me-mo.

hip, hop, pip, pop, tip, top, popcorn.

watt-what, wen-when, wine-whine, wear-where, wile-while, wet-whet, wit-whit, weal-wheel, wist-whist, weather-whether.

c. Open the jaw about two finger-widths and say slowly;

mah, bah, pah, testing the open position by measurement or with a mirror. Follow with rah, rah, rah, etc.

d. Imagine the tongue is sharpened to a point and pronounce:

> do, di, di, di, di
> dah, da, do, di
> tah, ta, to, ti
> lah, la, lo, li
> le, le, le, le, le, le
> li, li, li, li, li, li
> lo, lo, lo, lo, lo, lo
> loo, loo, loo, loo, loo, loo.

e. Till the tongue of fancy tingles with the tang of muscadine.

Thou testy little dogmatist, thou pretty katy-did.

Two toads totally tired trying to trot to Tadbury.

Oh, the terrible, tyrannous, treacherous Turk.

CHAPTER XI

Earning the Right to Speak

AFTER BECOMING PRESIDENT, Abraham Lincoln once said, "I believe that I shall never be old enough to speak without embarrassment when I have nothing to say." No man has the right to stand before an audience and consume its time without careful and painstaking preparation. He must earn the right to speak. There are those who aspire to speak impromptu (on the sudden); but there is no such thing as speaking "on the sudden," if that means speaking without preparation. Impromptu speaking occasionally becomes necessary in an emergency, but even then the speaker must rely upon earlier preparation. No man can speak without having something to say. It is impossible to draw water out of an empty well. Most impromptu attempts result in the haphazard, rambling, pointless type of speech that is embarrassing to all concerned.

The only defensible speech is one that is the product of thorough preparation. The price that must be paid for the privilege of standing before an audience is work—long and thorough study. No speaker has ever achieved success without it. Neither shall we. If you are not willing to work, speaking is not for you. It is said that Henry Ward Beecher had some sermons in mind more than forty years before he was ready to preach them. Webster's great Reply to Hayne in the United States Senate had been in the making at least twoscore years. On another occasion Webster said, "I would rather stand before an audience half-clothed than half-prepared." Among the ancient Greeks the famous orator Isocrates worked ten years to perfect a single speech; but the labor was worth while, for he sold it to a king for twenty talents of silver—the equivalent of $20,000. At least one modern-day American preacher gives twenty to thirty hours each week to preparing his Sunday sermon. Perhaps that is why a major radio network provides its coast-to-coast facilities free for the presentation.

Only the ignorant and the lazy try to speak without work. The wise know better. Here is the testimony of Alexander Hamilton:

Men give me some credit for genius. All the genius I have lies in this: When I have a subject in hand, I study it profoundly. Day and night it is before me. I explore it in all its bearings. My mind becomes pervaded with it. Then the efforts that I make are what people are pleased to call the fruits of genius. It is the fruit of labor and thought.

BEGIN EARLY—SPEECHES GROW

One of the most helpful suggestions that can be made to a beginning speaker is to *begin speech preparation early*. Speeches grow. They have a way of lying unnoticed in the subconscious mind, yet developing all the while. If the speaker will choose his subject several weeks before he plans to speak, he will be surprised at the number of ideas that will come his way without any effort. In an incident that occurs while he is driving through traffic he will see a wonderful illustration. As he listens to the radio he hears some facts or statistics which fit in. Conversation with a friend yields other valuable data. A magazine article provides an excellent quotation or two. The Sunday sermon has exactly the right Bible passage. Begin early, and the work of gathering material almost takes care of itself.

On the other hand, the speaker who puts off his preparation until the last few hours often finds that the springs of imagination are dry. Under pressure he can think of nothing that seems appropriate.

Dwight L. Moody's method of sermon preparation is interesting:

When I choose a subject, I write the name of it on the outside of a large envelope. I have many such envelopes. If, when I am reading, I meet a good thing on any subject I am to speak on, I slip it into the right envelope, and let it lie there. I always carry a notebook, and if I hear anything in a sermon that will throw light on that subject, I put it down, and slip it into the envelope. Perhaps I let it lie there for a year or more. When I want a new sermon, I take everything that has been accumulating. Between what I find there and the results of my own study, I have material enough. Then, all the time I am going over my sermons, taking out a little here, adding a little there. In that way they never get old.

Not only does beginning on time bring in a wealth of material, but it seasons the material and gives the speaker a sureness and confidence in what he says. Oliver Wendell Holmes wrote:

Talk about those subjects you have had long in your mind, and listen to what others say about subjects you have studied but recently. Knowledge and timber shouldn't be much used till they are seasoned. . . . Put an idea into your intelligence and leave it there an hour, a day, a year, without ever having occasion to refer to it. When, at last, you return to it, you do not find it as it was when acquired. It has domiciliated itself, so to speak,—become at home,

—entered into relations with your other thoughts, and integrated itself with the whole fabric of the mind.[1]

THINK THE SUBJECT THROUGH

Even before beginning to gather materials the speaker—like a merchant ordering stock from the wholesaler—should take inventory of what he has on hand: he should canvass his own mind to see what he already knows of his subject. Thinking comes before reading. Not only is this logical and economical of time; it is a means of making sure that the final speech is really a product of the speaker himself and not merely the parroting of one or more articles or sermons he has read or heard. The major fault of beginning college speakers, in composition, is the tendency to read one magazine article and present it to the class as a speech. Beginning religious speakers and even some mature preachers have the same major fault: they read one religious article or sermon and use it as a talk or sermon of their own. Not only is this plagiarism, but it also lacks the quality of conviction which results when the materials come out of the speaker's own heart and mind.

Begin your preparation, then, by jotting down on paper every idea, quotation, example, illustration, or scripture pertaining to your subject that comes to mind. Some of the items will be discarded before the final outline takes form, but the quality of those that are used will be high. After listing everything you know on your subject, make a first arrangement of the items in some kind of speech plan. This *preliminary outline* will guide your reading and study. It will serve as a unifying force.

---

[1]Holmes, *The Autocrat of the Breakfast-Table,* p. 134.

GATHER ADDITIONAL MATERIAL

After you have inventoried the material you already have, and after you have drawn up a preliminary outline, you are ready for research. For what kind of material will you be looking? Alan Monroe makes the most helpful analysis of the various types or kinds of speech material:[2]

1. Explanation.
2. Analogy or comparison.
3. Illustrations (detailed examples).
   a. Hypothetical (imaginary but true to life).
   b. Factual (real incident).
4. Specific instances (undeveloped examples).
5. Facts and statistics.
6. Testimony or quotation.
7. Restatement.

Every speech should have a balanced spread of the kinds of material indicated. Explanation and restatement are necessary, but low in interest qualities. Illustrations add life and make the meaning clear. Use them copiously. Facts and quotations furnish the meat that makes a speech worth hearing. Use all these materials with variety.

There are three general sources to which the speaker may go for material:

1. **Observation.** By keeping his eyes and ears open the speaker may learn much. In fact, each of the five senses can contribute to man's general background of knowledge. Actually, many people see the events that happen about them continually without ever really seeing them. The habit of thoughtful observation must be cultivated. Solomon found inspiration

---

[2]From *Principles and Types of Speech* by Alan H. Monroe. Copyright, 1949, by Scott, Foresman and Company, and reprinted with their permission. P. 221.

for many of his proverbs among the animals (ants, conies, and the like) which he observed. His father, David, showed an intimate acquaintance with the starry heavens (Psalm 19) as also did Job (Job 38). Jesus' teachings abound in parables about farmers, shepherds, merchants, husbandmen, children, and many others. Everywhere we look, there are "sermons in stones" if we will only see them.

2. **Reading.** The newspapers, magazines, and books of modern times are vast storehouses of information. The Library of Congress has more than 8,000,000 books for our use, and thousands more pour off the presses of the nation every day. "Of making many books there is no end."[3] In addition, there are the magazines and newspapers and pamphlets which almost submerge a person in reading matter. Through the printed page we have access to the wisdom of all times and of all places. By this one medium we can conquer the oceans as well as the centuries and drink deep of the experiences and inspiration of other people and other ages. The speaker must read widely in order to keep his mind stocked with the information that he will continually need.

3. **Conversation.** Many additional ideas may be gathered through talking with family and friends. The exchange of viewpoints is extremely helpful. In conversation, the members of a group tend to pool all their resources of facts, illustrations, and convictions. This is an almost effortless way to gather material quickly, though it lacks the depth and accuracy, oftentimes, of materials gathered from reading. It usually provides information that is interesting, however, for it has been remembered by someone. The use of questions—both oral and written —can be helpful in gathering material for a speech. Letters and questionnaires are often of value in getting information.

---

[3]Ecclesiastes 12:12.

TAKING NOTES

Reading should begin with the general—sources that treat the subject in a broad way—and narrow down to sources that are detailed and exhaustive on the specific subject. It should be supplemented by a systematic taking of notes. What is read may soon be forgotten unless you have "the paper habit." Following are a few suggestions for note taking:

1. **Use large cards** (preferably 4 by 6 inches), because you will often need more space than smaller cards offer.

2. **Put each item on a separate card,** to simplify the later classifying and grouping of materials.

3. **Record all information accurately,** with the exact title of the source, author, page, issue, date, and any other information that may eventually be needed.

4. **Copy exact quotations.** These will be more valuable than abstract summaries.

5. **Classify each card with a heading** which indicates the exact type of material on the card. Usually this can be done best at the end of your reading.

6. **Use the following form:**

(Classification)	(Author)	(Source)
Conviction	G. Bromley Oxnam, Methodist Bishop, Past Pres. Fed. Counc. of Churches	*Preaching in a Revolutionary Age,* p. 17.

When the police captain whispered to the aged Polycarp, "But what harm is it to say, 'Lord Caesar' and to offer sacrifice . . . and be saved?" the old man replied, "If you vainly suppose that I will swear by the genius of Caesar, as you say, . . . listen plainly: I am a Christian."

IDEAL FILING SYSTEM

Every person who does much public speaking will need to have some kind of *filing system* that will preserve the materials gathered from time to time and allow them to be found when needed. The following suggestions may be helpful:

1. **Illustration file:** This is a permanent file of illustrations, quotations, poems, statistics, and proverbs. Using the form of the example above, it should be kept on 4- by-6-inch cards. Quality and not quantity should govern the selection of materials (illustration books can be bought, but their materials are never as valuable as those which are hand-picked). The gathering of items should continue throughout the speaker's life, so that when he wants something he can always find it in black and white.

2. **Subject file:** This is a permanent file of information, kept in 8½- by-11-inch Manila folders in a standard drawer file. The information (pamphlets, tracts, notes, outlines, etc.) is on every religious subject. Newspaper or magazine articles of special value can be clipped and dropped into the appropriate folder. It is a great help, in preparing to speak, to be able to go to a file and draw out a folder of information on the subject.

3. **Source file:** This contains sources of material on every religious subject. It, too, should be kept on 4- by-6-inch cards, since eventually each card may list many references. It guides the speaker to magazines or books which contain articles or chapters on a subject.

4. **Sermon file:** An outline of each talk or sermon should be preserved, either in the subject file described or in a special file or book. Occasions may arise when you will wish to use again part or all of some previously prepared outline. A record of where each talk was made should accompany the outline.

5. **Magazine file:** Many a speaker has some of his most valuable magazines bound in book form at the end of each year,

in order to have permanent use of them. The cost is usually nominal.

ACTIVITIES

1. Make a two-minute talk on some Biblical place or thing about which you have learned exclusively from reading—for example, the Cave of Machpelah.

2. Make a two-minute talk, drawn from observation exclusively.

3. Start you own filing system *now*.

CHAPTER XII

Organization and Arrangement

"THE COMMON ERROR in regard to speaking is the assumption that all that is necessary is to have 'something to say.' Utterly false! Unless that 'something to say' is said in accordance with the laws of the human mind which govern conviction, it might as well be spoken to the winds. . . . The modern speaker, then, must rid himself of the notion that 'something to say' is sufficient; that the impulsive utterance of an idea will of itself secure belief or action. He must realize that besides 'something to say' he must learn how best to convey it. He must remember that the Chathams and the Websters and the Beechers not only had 'something to say,' but that they realized that careful study had to be given to the order and manner of its presentation."[1]

The beginning speaker often feels that building a careful outline or plan is unnecessary. He fails to realize that the outline is to a speech what the skeleton is to a human body, or

---

[1]Arthur Edward Phillips, *Effective Speaking* (Chicago: The Newton Company, 1938), pp. 14–15.

what the blueprint is to a builder. Without the bony structure man's body would be a jellylike mass, incapable of any worthwhile activity. Almost the same can be said of a speech that has no plan. It is likely to remind the audience of the "horseman who mounted his steed and rode off in all directions." Many a speaker has started without knowing where he is going, and has finished without knowing where he has been.

As long ago as Aristotle, three centuries before Christ, there was a continual emphasis upon the necessity of a plan or outline. Aristotle's division was into two main parts: proposition and proof. The Roman, Quintilian, suggested a fivefold organizational plan which was followed by writers for several centuries after his day: (1) exordium, (2) statement of facts, (3) proof, (4) refutation, and (5) peroration. The apostle Paul gave the advice, "Let all things be done decently and in order."[2] Almost without exception great speakers—Daniel Webster, Wendell Phillips, Henry W. Grady, Henry Ward Beecher, William Jennings Bryan, and Abraham Lincoln, to name only a few—have ordered their thoughts by an outline. In the beginning years the outline should be carefully worked out on paper; maybe in later years the mature, experienced speaker can work it out in his head. Maybe!

THE TRADITIONAL OUTLINE

Of the two basic plans of speech organization discussed in this chapter the traditional plan is by far the more widely used and the more generally useful. It has been standardized quite generally so that rules for constructing it can be named:

1. **Begin with your proposition.** Having a "purpose sentence" before you the entire time of preparation, you are more likely to achieve your goal.

---

[2] I Corinthians 14:40.

2. **Divide your outline into three major parts:** *Introduction, Discussion, and Conclusion.* Each major division of the speech should be marked by inserting the word "Introduction" or "Discussion" or "Conclusion" in the center of the page. Each division will have its own distinct, separate set of numbers. The Introduction will have its own I, II, III, as needed, while the Discussion will have its own I, II, III, as needed, and the Conclusion also will have a I, II, III.

3. **Include only one item or statement in each unit.** The relationship between items in the outline can be shown only if each item is separate. Never say:

I. The Jordan River is interesting both because of its history and because of its physical make-up.

Instead, say:

I. The Jordan River is interesting because of its history.

II. The Jordan River is interesting because of its physical make-up.

4. **Select a consistent set of symbols to show the relationship between main points and subordinate points.** The most common and perhaps the best system is as follows:

I.
    A.
       1.
          a.
             (I)
                (A).
                (B).
             (II).
          b.
       2.
    B.
II.

5. **Show the relationship between main points and subordinate points by proper indentation.** An indentation of three spaces is usually satisfactory.

6. **Use complete sentences for all main headings and subheadings.** Full sentences make the outline more intelligible. They also insure that the speaker himself will remember the materials of the speech at some later time. Some months after use an item listed simply as "Illustration of the dog" is likely to be meaningless. Use a complete sentence.

7. **Phrase each statement as it is to be spoken to the audience.** Instead of saying, "Tell them about the example of Joseph," say, "Joseph was always true to his convictions." This makes for a better style in the speech, which does not have to be translated into different words before being delivered.

Correct outlining requires a disciplining of the mind, but speakers must pay this price for effectiveness. Alert, ambitious speakers are happy to pay it. Lazy, indolent speakers prefer to get by with less effort. At first, the process may seem to be a bit difficult; but careful adherence to these rules through the early years of a speaking career will be deeply rewarding later when the system becomes habitual and easy.

SAMPLE OF THE TRADITIONAL OUTLINE

THE FIRST COMMANDMENT

Proposition: "To lead men to want to give themselves completely into the service of God."

Introduction

I. On one occasion a scribe came to Jesus to ask: "What commandment is the first of all?"

II. Jesus answered, "The first is, Hear, O Israel; The Lord our God, the Lord is one: and thou shalt love the Lord thy

God with all thy heart, and with all thy soul, and with all thy mind, and with all thy strength." (Mark 12:28–30.)

Discussion

I. Thou shalt love the Lord thy God with all thy mind.
  A. Mind refers to the intellect, the thinking part of man.
  B. Man must devote his mind to a careful study of the scriptures to learn what God's will is.
    1. Acts 17:11.
    2. II Timothy 2:15.
    3. Titus 1:9; 2:1.
  C. But man must not stop with an intellectual understanding of the word of God lest his religion be cold and formal.

II. Thou shalt love the Lord thy God with all thy heart.
  A. Heart refers to the feelings and emotions of man.
  B. With the heart man loves his wife and children.
  C. David is an example of a man who loved God with his heart, as the many moving passages in the Psalms plainly show.
  D. Heart alone is dangerous in religion.
    1. It leads one to be very spiritual and to feel very deeply, but
    2. It often tends toward a carelessness about obeying the commands of the Lord.

III. Thou shalt love the Lord thy God with all thy soul.
  A. The soul is more difficult to define than mind or heart.
  B. The scriptures often translate the word "psyche," used here, by the word "life" instead of "soul."
    1. Matthew 6:25.
    2. Mark 3:4.
    3. John 15:13.
    4. Matthew 20:28.

C. We must love God to the extent of our soul, or life, or breath.

IV. Thou shalt love the Lord thy God with all thy strength.

    A. Strength refers to talents, abilities, and energies.

    B. We must be willing to spend and be spent in the Lord's service.

       1. Romans 12:1.

       2. I Corinthians 6:19–20.

Conclusion

I. We must love God with all that is in us; part will not do.

II. There is a great difference in men at the time when they become Christians.

    A. Some are merely obeying commandments.

    B. Others are giving themselves to the Lord.

III. This is the greatest commandment of all.

THE MOTIVATED SEQUENCE OUTLINE

The second of the two major approaches to outlining grows out of the way man thinks. According to the noted educator John Dewey:

> Upon examination, each instance of reflective thought reveals more or less clearly, five logically distinct steps: (1) a felt difficulty; (2) its location and definition; (3) suggestion of possible solution; (4) development by reasoning of the bearings of the suggestion; (5) further observation and experiment leading to its acceptance or rejection.[3]

Alan Monroe has made a valuable adaptation of the principle contained in this quotation to speechmaking. He explains, "This form of speech structure we shall call *the motivated sequence: the sequence of ideas which, by following the normal*

---

[3]*How We Think* (Boston: D. C. Heath and Company, 1910), p. 72. Used by permission.

process of human thinking, motivates the audience to respond to the speaker's purpose."[4] He then proceeds to suggest this plan:

I. *Attention Step.* To secure the attention of the audience.

II. *Need Step.* To define the problem and to focus the attention of the audience upon the fact that something must be done.

III. *Satisfaction Step.* To name possible solutions to the problem, and to point out the best of the available solutions.

IV. *Visualization Step.* To carry out the proposed solution, in the mind, demonstrating its virtues.

V. *Action Step.* To appeal for acceptance and action on the part of the audience.

Dr. Monroe's organizational plan is effective where there is a problem to be solved. In other cases the traditional plan is more appropriate. Neither should be used exclusively, for there is a definite need for both approaches to speech organization.

SAMPLE OF THE MOTIVATED SEQUENCE OUTLINE

"E PLURIBUS UNUM"

Proposition: "To lead all believers in Christ to want to unite in Christ's church."

Attention Step: I. There are too many churches in America.

A. At first this sounds like the expression of a critic of religion.

B. The speaker, however, is in full sympathy with true Christianity.

[4]From *Principles and Types of Speech* by Alan H. Monroe. Copyright, 1949, by Scott, Foresman and Company, and reprinted with their permission. P. 309 ff.

II. We are concerned to find the reasons why, after more than sixty generations of time, Christianity is no more effective in America than it is.

Need Step: I. The church is divided.
   A. The official United States Census Reports give the following facts:
      1. 1906—191 religious bodies.
      2. 1916—202 religious bodies
      3. 1926—215 religious bodies.
      4. 1936—256 religious bodies.
   B. It is estimated that there are now more than 300 separate churches in America.

II. Christ desired that all believers be one.
   A. John 17:20-23.
   B. I Corinthians 1:10-13.

III. Religious division has hindered the progress of Christianity.
   A. Wars are still raging throughout the world.
   B. Crime and vice are still running rampant.
   C. Infidelity is still common.

Satisfaction Step: I. "E Pluribus Unum" suggests the answer.
   A. The meaning of this motto of the United States is "From many into one."

B. We need to do in the religious world what the early American colonies did in the political world.
   1. In unity there is strength.
   2. A handful of sand is impotent —but bind the grains of sand together with some cohesive force, and they become a rock.

II. Why not unite on the church described in the Bible?
   A. It would have an appeal to all God-fearing people.
   B. It would have the approval of God and Christ.
   C. Let us leave man-made creeds.
   D. Let us "speak where the Bible speaks and be silent where the Bible is silent."

Visualization Step: I. The restoration of New Testament Christianity has already begun.
   A. Hundreds of thousands of believers in Christ have already pledged themselves to return to the church of the apostolic age.
   B. Several thousand congregations of the New Testament church already exist in America.

II. The Restoration movement, begun a century and a half ago, is making greater progress today than ever before.

Action Step: I. Let each man study his Bible to discover the Lord's church.

II. Let each man give himself, his ener-
gies, his talents, and his wealth to the
triumph of Christ's church.

ACTIVITIES

1. Bring to class an outline you have made yourself according
to the instructions given in this chapter.

2. Ask some experienced speaker to show you his system of
making outlines.

3. Make a careful outline for each of your speeches in the
future.

CHAPTER XIII

Beginning and Ending the Speech

THE MOST EMPHATIC parts of a speech are the beginning and the end. An excellent beginning goes a long way toward making an effective speech, and a strong conclusion may turn the tide in winning the desired audience response. There is an old saying about actors: "By their entrances and their exits shall ye know them." Speakers sometimes underrate these parts of the speech and consequently neglect them. Many a sermon is worked out with great care until the conclusion is reached, and then is left to take care of itself. It is wise to master the technique of beginning and ending speeches with strength, for no position in the speech is quite so strategic as are these two.

THE INTRODUCTION

Purposes: In the beginning the speaker's first desire is to get the *attention* of his hearers. Without attention nothing he says will be of any value whatsoever. Dale Carnegie writes:

I once asked Dr. Lynn Harold Hough, formerly president of Northwestern University, what was the most important fact that his long experience as a speaker had taught him. After pondering for a minute, he replied, "To get an arresting opening, something that will seize the attention immediately." He plans in advance almost the precise words of both his opening and closing. John Bright did the same thing. Gladstone did it. Webster did it. Lincoln did it. Practically every speaker with common sense and experience does it.[1]

To speak without first opening the listener's ears is much like beginning to talk over a telephone before the person at the other end has picked up the receiver. In addition to initial attention, the speaker desires the *good will* of his auditors: he wants them not only to listen but to be glad that they are listening. In addition to attenion and good will he wants *respect,* for the best results come only when the audience feels that the speaker deserves to be heard, and that he has something worth while to give. Finally, the introduction needs to *lead into the subject.* Many times the subject requires explanation or clarification, and often the audience needs to be told why the subject is important at this time. Certain terms may need to be defined before the speaker launches out. All of this is the work of the introduction.

Types of Introduction: While there are many approaches to the beginning of a speech, the following are the most common and also the most effective:

(1) **Quotation.** An appropriate scripture passage is probably the most effective means of beginning a religious talk. Although it has been used from time immemorial, it is still good. Other types of quotation also are often used. When Harry Emerson Fosdick addressed the League of Nations Assembly

[1]Carnegie, *Public Speaking, and Influencing Men in Business* (New York: The Association Press, 1937), p. 187. Used by permission.

Service at Geneva in 1925, he spoke on "A Christian Conscience About War" and began with the words, "All they that take the sword shall perish with the sword."[2]

(2) **Illustration.** Illustrations create real situations and paint vivid mental pictures, and so they are splendid beginning materials. Any real-life situation tends to create interest. Take the opening paragraph of Russell H. Conwell's *Acres of Diamonds:*

When going down the Tigris and Euphrates rivers many years ago with a party of English travelers I found myself under the direction of an old Arab guide whom we hired up at Bagdad . . . He thought that it was not only his duty to guide us down those rivers, and do what he was paid for doing, but also to entertain us with stories curious and weird, ancient and modern, strange and familiar. Many of them I have forgotten, and I am glad I have, but there is one I shall never forget.[3]

This sort of beginning whets the appetite for more.

(3) **Questions.** Another of the better ways of beginning a speech is through the use of rhetorical questions. Such questions effectively direct the attention of the audience to the subject. Of course the speaker does not expect an answer, and rather proceeds to answer the questions in the course of his speech. The question technique was used some years ago by Robert M. Hutchins, Chancellor of the University of Chicago, when he said, "The great problems before us are, first, can we survive, and second, what kind of life are we going to lead if we do?"[4]

(4) **Reference to the Subject** to be discussed, although not especially strong as a way of securing attention, is an oft-used

[2]Matthew 26:52.
[3]Conwell, *Acres of Diamonds* (New York: Harper & Brothers, 1915), p. 3. Used by permission.
[4]A. Craig Baird, editor, *Representative American Speeches, 1945–46,* p. 262.

introduction technique. Wendell Phillips's famous "Eulogy on Daniel O'Connell" begins with the words, "A hundred years ago today Daniel O'Connell was born."[5] Immediately, he came to his theme—the honoring of O'Connell.

(5) **Reference to Occasion or Setting.** Sometimes the occasion itself is foremost in the thoughts of the audience. Then it is often wise for the speaker to open by referring to the occasion. At other times the physical setting of the speech is so prominent that reference to it is natural and desirable. Some years ago Douglas Horton began his famous sermon, "Taking a City," by reference to the city of Chicago in which it was delivered:

> Over against us looms this magnificent and terrible city of Chicago. Our problem is how to convert this city, stupendous as it is, into the still more stupendous city of God. . . . How shall we make the city not merely hog butcher, tool maker, and emporium for commerce, but also a reservoir of humanity at its best, a city which clothes all of its citizens in faith, a city where the good life is lived naturally and all men know the meaning of liberty and loyalty? How, in a word, shall we impart a soul to Chicago?"[6]

(6) **Reference to Self.** The personal introduction is often over-used, but is defensible under certain circumstances. When the audience is thinking more about the speaker than about the occasion or the subject, it may be appropriate for the speaker to begin with a reference to himself. Clarence Darrow made such an introduction to his famous defense of Loeb and Leopold in a Chicago court in 1924:

---

[5]William N. Brigance, *Classified Speech Models* (New York: F. S. Crofts & Co., 1930), p. 374. Used by permission of Appleton-Century-Crofts, Inc.

[6]Douglas Horton, *Taking a City* (New York: Harper & Brothers, 1934). Quoted by Andrew W. Blackwood, *The Protestant Pulpit* (New York: Abingdon-Cokesbury Press, 1947), p. 205.

Your Honor, it has been almost three months since the great responsibility of this case was assumed by my associates and myself. I am willing to confess that it has been three months of great anxiety. A burden which I gladly would have been spared excepting for my feeling of affection toward some of the members of one of the unfortunate families. This responsibility is almost too great for any one to assume; but we lawyers can no more choose than the court can choose.[7]

The personal introduction should never resolve itself into the overworked "I am glad to be here." It should never be an apology, and it must always be within the bounds of modesty. (7) **Unusual or Startling Statement.** Occasionally there is a place for something startling or unusual. A striking example is that of the speaker who began:

"I believe it is the historic mission of the laboring class to destroy every vestige of capitalism! I hold in contempt all the institutions of capitalism . . . its laws, its flag, its courts, its churches, and its religion!"

He paused, and then continued:

Are you appalled at such words? . . . You may well be! You have just listened to the basic doctrine and the attending oath of allegiance of the Industrial Workers of the World. They are words of treason![8]

Or perhaps you have heard of the sermon which began with a string of profanity. The congregation sat in shocked silence. Then, the preacher continued, "On my way here I heard a man say those words." He had introduced his sermon on profanity, though there might be reasonable question about the propriety

---

[7]Brigance, *op. cit.*, p. 137.

[8]Brigance, *Speech Composition* (New York: F. S. Crofts & Co., 1937), p. 127. Used by permission of Appleton-Century-Crofts, Inc.

of such a potent beginning. Religious speaking should not cater to sensationalism.

CONCLUSIONS

Purposes. After the body of the speech there needs to be a *rounding out of the thought,* a summing up of what has been said. This is the work of the conclusion. Either formally or informally, the speaker may *summarize* what he has said; or he may simply choose to *focus the attention of the audience on his central theme* or proposition. Nearly always he will include an *appeal* for some kind of response. It may be that he wants the hearers actually to do something, such as to accept Christ as their Savior and to obey the commands of the Gospel. The appeal for response must be very clear and forceful.

Types of Conclusion. The following types are among the most commonly and effectively used:

(1) **Summary.** Speeches in which close reasoning and careful arguments have been presented often benefit from a formal summary—listing the major points in the exact words in which they have already appeared. More often an informal summary, such as the one used by Dr. Arthur H. Compton before the American Physical Society, is appropriate:

> In summary, therefore, I would note that by far the most significant direct social effect of the release of atomic energy is to unite the world in an effort to eliminate war. We have reason to hope that this effort may be successful.[9]

(2) **Illustration.** An illustration which fits the situation exactly is a telling way to conclude a speech. An address on the great need for proper care and guidance in the rearing of children concluded with the story of a boy who had great difficulty in

---

[9]Baird, *op. cit.,* p. 119.

learning geography. His father bought a map of the world, brought it home, tore it into irregular pieces, and challenged him to put it together again by offering him five dollars. In an amazingly short time, the boy had put the map together. The father asked how he had done it. The boy confided that there was a picture of a boy on the back of the map, and he had thought, "If I put the boy together right, the world will take care of itself." Such a story may be the making of a speech.

(3) **Quotation.** An apt quotation which epitomizes the message of the entire speech may be the most effective type of conclusion. At the already mentioned League of Nations Assembly Service, Harry Emerson Fosdick began with the words, "All they that take the sword shall perish with the sword." He concluded with the same epigrammatic sentence.

(4) **Personal Reference.** Although personal references should be used sparingly and judiciously, one may be very forceful. Could there be a better conclusion to Joshua's farewell address in the long ago:

And if it seem evil unto you to serve Jehovah, choose you this day whom ye will serve; whether the gods which your fathers served that were beyond the River, or the gods of the Amorites, in whose land ye dwell: but as for me and my house, we will serve Jehovah.[10]

(5) **Appeal for Action.** After carefully building to a climax, a speaker will often want to appeal for some specific action. In the greatest sermon of all time, Jesus used this type of conclusion:

Every one therefore that heareth these words of mine, and doeth them, shall be likened unto a wise man, who built his house upon the rock: and the rain descended, and the floods came, and the

---

[10]Joshua 24:15.

winds blew, and beat upon that house; and it fell not: for it was founded upon the rock. And every one that heareth these words of mine, and doeth them not, shall be likened unto a foolish man, who built his house upon the sand: and the rain descended, and the floods came, and the winds blew, and smote upon that house; and it fell: and great was the fall thereof.[11]

The wise speaker carefully plans his speech to accomplish the purpose which he has chosen, then gives special attention to getting it off to a good start and to closing it with force and power. The old adage, "It's the little things that count," might well be applied to the often neglected introduction and conclusion. They are relatively brief—not more than two or three minutes each in a half-hour address—but they are none the less important. It is not out of place to suggest here that brevity in the entire speech is usually a virtue. Get a good beginning and a good ending, and get them close together. At least one African tribe allows a man to speak only as long as he can stand on one foot: when the other foot touches the ground he must quit. And we are all familiar with the old saw, "A speech does not need to be eternal in order to be immortal."

ACTIVITIES

1. Choose some theme for a speech. Without building the entire speech, plan an effective introduction. Tell the class your theme, then introduce it.

2. Work out only the conclusion for some speech theme. Tell the class the substance of the imaginary speech, then deliver your conclusion.

3. Make an oral report of introductions and conclusions that you have heard various speakers use.

4. Study several written speeches from the standpoint of the

---

[11]Matthew 7:24–27.

introduction and conclusion. References to collections of speeches may be found in this chapter and in the Bibliography at the end of the book. Most well equipped libraries also carry the magazine *Vital Speeches of the Day.*

5. Check the *Reader's Digest* for the techniques of the various writers in opening and closing their articles.

CHAPTER XIV

Persuasion

PERSUASIVENESS IS THE skill for which the highest premiums are paid. No other skill is so widely sought in management, labor, salesmanship, education, politics, statesmanship, or any other field in which men work together; and no gift is more needed in the Lord's work than the ability to influence others. The art of influencing people—possibly it could more accurately be called a science, because it is regulated by an extensive body of rules—is known as *persuasion.* An understanding of the principles of persuasion is essential to an effective speaker for the Lord.

ETHICAL PERSUASION

Through many pages we have been studying the techniques of good speaking, but here come to what William Norwood Brigance calls the "Great First Cause"—the speaker himself. *Ethical persuasion* lies in the speaker as a person. It includes what the audience knows of him before he rises to speak: his reputation for honesty, integrity, good will, and other such factors. It includes his appearance and grooming. It includes also what he displays during his speech: his background of information, his wisdom, his trustworthiness, and his attitude toward the audience. If he could, miraculously, be brought back to life, the apostle Paul, for example, would be a man of extremely high ethical persuasion.

Three centuries before Christ, Aristotle wrote:

The proofs provided through the instrumentality of the speech are of three kinds, consisting either in the moral character of the speaker or in the production of a certain disposition in the audience or in the speech itself by means of real or apparent demonstration. The instrument of proof is the moral character, when the delivery of the speech is such as to produce an impression of the speaker's credibility; for we yield a more complete and ready credence to persons of high character not only ordinarily and in a general way, but in such matters as do not admit of absolute certainty but necessarily leave room for difference of opinion, without any qualification whatever.[1]

In effect Aristotle is saying that there is no proof so forceful as character. The three factors which influence belief most, according to the same writer, are *sagacity, high character,* and *good will.* Isocrates, another ancient Greek, wrote in the *Antidosis:*

Furthermore, the man who wishes to persuade people will not be negligent as to the matter of character; no, on the contrary, he will apply himself above all to establish a most honourable name among his fellow citizens, for who does not know that words carry greater conviction when spoken by men of good repute than when spoken by men who live under a cloud, and that the argument which is made by a man's life is of more weight than that which is

---

[1]Aristotle, *The Rhetoric of Aristotle,* p. 10.

furnished by words? Therefore the stronger a man's desire to persuade his hearers, the more zealously will he strive to be honourable and to have the esteem of his fellow-citizens.

Ralph Waldo Emerson wrote not only, "What you are speaks so loud I cannot hear what you say," but also, "The reason why anyone refuses his assent to your opinion, or his aid to your benevolent design, is in you. He refuses to accept you as a bringer of truth, because . . . you have not given him the authentic sign."[2]

In 1858 when Lincoln and Douglas made their debating tour in Illinois, the people called them "honest Abe" and "the little giant." It was Lincoln that they eventually sent to the White House. Carlyle said, "I should say sincerity, a great deep, genuine sincerity, is the first characteristic of all men in any way heroic." It is interesting to find in Dale Carnegie's famous book *Public Speaking, and Influencing Men in Business:*

The finest thing in speaking is neither physical nor mental. It is spiritual. The Book that Daniel Webster had on his pillow while dying is a book that every speaker should have on his desk while living.

Jesus loved men and their hearts burned within them as He talked with them by the way. If you want a splendid text on public speaking, why not read your New Testament?[3]

Particularly is it true of religious speaking that high moral character is an absolute prerequisite to effectiveness. In all public speaking it is a significant item, but in the kind of speaking with which this book is concerned it is the very foundation. *A speaker must have the confidence of the people before he can persuade.*

---

[2] Emerson, *Journals,* Vol. IX, p. 342 (quoted in Thonssen and Baird, *Speech Criticism,* p. 383).

[3] Carnegie, *Public Speaking, and Influencing Men in Business* (New York: The Association Press, 1937), p. 113. Used by permission.

SECURING ATTENTION

In the speech, the first step toward persuading an audience is to secure attention—not just any kind of attention, but *fair, favorable,* and *undivided* attention. Attention may be of several varieties. *Voluntary attention* is given because of a sense of duty. *Involuntary attention* is given to some spectacular occurrence, such as the passing of a fire engine. *Nonvoluntary attention* is given because of intrinsic interest in a subject; and of course this is the only type of attention that a speaker really wants.

The art of securing fair, favorable, and undivided attention is a matter for serious study. Alan Monroe[4] lists nine "factors of attention" which are believed to be capable of capturing the spontaneous attention of an audience:

1. Activity or Movement.   4. Familiarity.   7. Conflict.
2. Reality.   5. Novelty.   8. Humor.
3. Proximity.   6. Suspense.   9. The Vital.

People are most interested in what concerns them personally. Lord Northcliffe, the British newspaper publisher, once said that people are more interested in "themselves" than in anything else. The average man is more disturbed about a dull razor blade than about a revolt in Indo-China. The cook's leaving is more significant than the United Nations. He is more concerned about a toothache than about a million-dollar fire in a distant state. We are concerned most with something that affects us personally. That always gets our attention.

AROUSING DESIRES

Experience has taught that each of us has many basic human urges or drives, sometimes called instincts, emotions, habitual

[4]From *Principles and Types of Speech* by Alan H. Monroe. Copyright, 1949, by Scott, Foresman and Company, and reprinted with their permission. P. 252.

action tendencies. To recognize these basic motives is simply to recognize the way we are made. They are neither bad nor good in themselves, but can be used either for worth-while purposes or for unworthy purposes. The public speaker who wishes to persuade must learn what these inner drives are and adapt his appeals to them. Oversimplifying the process, we may compare persuasion to the pushing of the right buttons on a cash register. If you want the dollar sign, push the button for the dollar sign. If you want to record a dime, the dime button is the one to push. Make the right appeals, and the audience responds.

In a rather broad grouping of "impelling wants" Brigance[5] lists the four major areas:

1. Protective wants.
2. Acquisitive wants.
3. Social wants.
4. Sensory wants.

Monroe[6] gives a more detailed listing under "types of motive appeals":

1. Acquisition and saving.
2. Adventure.
3. Companionship.
4. Creating.
5. Curiosity.
6. Destruction.
7. Fear.
8. Fighting.
9. Imitation.
10. Independence.
11. Loyalty.
12. Personal enjoyment.
13. Power and authority.
14. Pride.
15. Reverence or worship.
16. Revulsion.
17. Sex attraction.
18. Sympathy.

How are these appeals used? Notice a few practical examples. A father discovers that his teen-age boy is surreptitiously smoking cigarettes. He could scold and threaten the boy, but it would not accomplish his desired goal. Instead, he

[5] Brigance, *Speech Composition* (New York: F. S. Crofts & Co., 1937), pp. 121–122. Used by permission of Appleton-Century-Crofts, Inc.
[6] Monroe, *op. cit.,* p. 196.

patiently shows the boy that smoking will reduce his chance of making the first string on the football squad. If he can persuade the boy that smoking will prevent his achieving some cherished goal there will be no smoking.

On Mars' Hill in ancient Athens the apostle Paul did not endeavor to batter down the convictions of the pagans. Instead, he began:

Ye men of Athens, in all things I perceive that ye are very religious. For as I passed along, and observed the objects of your worship, I found also an altar with this inscription, TO AN UNKNOWN GOD. What therefore ye worship in ignorance, this I set forth unto you.[7]

He began with something they already accepted, and revealed to them "the unknown God." When he finished some believed and others said, "We will hear thee concerning this yet again."

When Jacob sent his sons into Egypt to buy grain from Pharaoh, he said, "Take of the choice fruits of the land in your vessels, and carry down the man a present, a little balm, and a little honey, spicery and myrrh, nuts, and almonds."[8] He was paving the way for his urgent request through the use of these basic appeals.

To achieve a high degree of effectiveness in persuading hearers, one must learn to appeal in terms of these basic motives or desires, most of which yield themselves either directly or indirectly to the high purposes of the religious speaker, though some are less suited than others. Here a paragraph from Ralph Sockman is interesting:

In a religious journal [*Zion's Herald,* March 13 and 27, 1940], a specialist in business salesmanship essayed recently to advise the pulpit how it could reach a larger public by appealing to the twelve basic emotional hungers which the business world capitalizes. He

[7]Acts 17:22–23.
[8]Genesis 43:11.

listed these hungers as follows: security, progress, health and beauty, superiority, companionship, acquisition, activity, competition, group urge as in family and race, curiosity, sex, and religion. That people will go where they think these hungers can be satisfied, is not to be denied.[9]

DEFINITION OF PERSUASION

Now that we have made a somewhat detailed analysis of what is involved in persuasion, perhaps we are ready for a definition. Brigance defines it: "When the aim is to rouse from indifference, to inspire, or to stimulate lagging enthusiasms and faiths, persuasion is a process of vitalizing old desires, purposes, or ideals. When the aim is to secure the acceptance of new beliefs or courses of action, persuasion is a process of substituting new desires, purposes, or ideals for old ones."[10]

ACTIVITIES

1. Each student should choose a theme with which he feels that others may disagree. He should then prepare the material of the speech with the primary thought of winning their approval. Do not argue; persuade.

2. Choose from some popular magazine or newspaper several examples of appeals to the various basic human desires, and bring them to class. Pictures, editorials, or advertising copy may be used. Analyze the appeals in terms of the materials in this chapter.

---

[9]Sockman, *The Highway of God* (New York: The Macmillan Company, 1942), pp. 35–36. Used by permission.
[10]Brigance, *op. cit.,* p. 139.

CHAPTER XV

Words

WORDS ARE THE tools with which the speaker works. They are the bridges over which his ideas are transported into the minds of his hearers. "He who wants to persuade," said Joseph Conrad, "should put his trust not in the right argument, but in the right word. . . . Give me the right word and the right accent, and I will move the world."[1] The study of the use of words, or style, is a vital matter to every speaker, as William Pierson Merrill pointed out to preachers:

A good English style is as essential to the preacher as a good delivery wagon is to the grocer. There are too many men in the pulpit who know a good deal, and think well enough, but have never gained the mastery of effective and simple language, through much companionship with the best writers, through deliberate and painstaking cultivation of a homely forceful use of words. A preacher without skill in words is like a knight with no knowledge of sword play.[2]

---

[1] As quoted in William N. Brigance, *Speech Composition* (New York: F. S. Crofts & Co., 1937), p. 199. Used by permission of Appleton-Century-Crofts, Inc.

[2] William Pierson Merrill, *The Freedom of the Preacher,* p. 34.

Perhaps a definition of "style" is in order at this point. Paul Scherer's definition will serve:

"Style" is not a mysterious something that you acquire only after years of laborious and painstaking effort; style is merely the way you have of expressing yourself. Your style may be good; it may be bad: but you have it already. You can change it for a better, or you can let it get altogether out of hand, if you like, and flop over into something that is worse. But you already have it. Improving it, strengthening it, beautifying it, pointing it, is no end of good sport. Forcing ideas to associate or come apart, bullying stubborn words to assume a certain pattern, all the fun, as someone has said, of being a dictator without any of the risks.[3]

Charles Reynolds Brown called attention to the fact that as long ago as the time of Augustine the three most desirable qualities of style were clearness, force, and beauty. He then added, "The best style for public address is one which makes your thought presentable, interesting, effective, without ever attracting the attention of the people to itself."[4]

VIVIDNESS

No quality of style is more important than vividness, the quality of putting your message into such form that it will capture your hearers' attention and imbed itself deeply in their minds. It must always be concrete and specific. As Howard Crosby pointed out:

Men are taught best, as children are, by object lessons, and if the object may not be actually seen, it can be described. A sermon of mere abstractions may do for the trained thinker, but as the vast

---

[3]Scherer, *For We Have This Treasure* (New York: Harper & Brothers, 1944), p. 186. Used by permission.
[4]Brown, *The Art of Preaching* (New York: The Macmillan Company, 1922), pp. 4–5, 177. Used by permission.

majority of men are not trained thinkers, it is most important to reduce the abstract as far as possible to the concrete.[5]

In the words of Henry Ward Beecher, "That which will touch men most sensibly, and arouse them most effectively, and bring them to a new life most certainly, is that which is specific."[6] Notice an example of this. In describing the size of the atom, Sir Oliver Lodge told his audience, "There are as many atoms in a single drop of water as there are drops of water in the Mediterranean Sea, or as there are blades of grass on the entire earth."

Christ used parables extensively to convey most profound truths. The story of the Good Samaritan, the story of the Prodigal Son, and the Parable of the Sower have made deep impressions on countless millions of people. They are clear, powerful, and easily remembered. Illustrations serve as windows to let light into speeches. In addition, they are in such form as to create a mental picture that is concrete and specific. The four chief reasons for the use of illustrations are:

1. They make the speaker's meaning clear.
2. They help the listeners remember.
3. They exert a force of proof or persuasion.
4. They awaken and sustain interest.

Of course they should not be used for their own sake. In preparing a speech, begin with a message, and then let illustrations help put it over.

The famous proverbs of man are also pictorial and vivid; for example, "Don't swap horses in the middle of the stream," "A bird in the hand is worth two in the bush," "You can lead a horse to water, but you can't make him drink," and "It never rains but it pours." Each of these creates a picture. The same is true of good slogans: "Watch the Fords go by," "Ivory soap

[5]Crosby, *The Christian Preacher,* pp. 65–66.
[6]Beecher, *Yale Lectures on Preaching,* Vol. III, p. 215.

is 99 44/100 per cent pure—it floats," and "The pause that refreshes." We have already mentioned the proverb, "One picture is worth a thousand words."

As R. W. Dale pointed out, "Monotony is almost always fatal to interest; monotony of voice, monotony of style, monotony of intellectual activity."[7] Illustrations aid greatly in breaking it. While a speaker must strive to be so interesting that his hearers find it difficult to think of anything else, sensationalism is to be avoided. There is an old saying, "To attract attention: first, be smart; if you can't be smart, be shrewd; if you can't be shrewd, be loud." This kind of attention-getting has no place in religious speaking.

WORD CHOICE

In the selection of the words to be spoken the following qualities should be kept in mind:

1. **Clearness.** Words should be transparent, calling no attention to themselves, so that the ideas they express shine through them without being colored or distorted.

2. **Simplicity.** Young speakers feel it advisable occasionally to use the biggest and most impressive words at their command. The advice of the apostle Paul is appropriate here: "unless ye utter by the tongue speech easy to be understood, how shall it be known what is spoken? for ye will be speaking into the air."[8] A word count of the American Revised translation of Christ's "Sermon on the Mount" shows that just under seventy-nine per cent of the words were of one syllable, seventeen per cent were of two syllables, and just over four per cent were of three or more syllables. Addressing college sophomores, William Jennings Byran said:

Our use of big words increases from infancy to the day of grad-

---

[7]Dale, *Nine Lectures on Preaching*, p. 33.
[8]I Corinthians 14:9.

uation. I think it is safe to say that with nearly all of us the maximum is reached on the day when we leave school. We use more big words that day than we have ever used before or will ever use again. When we go from college into everyday life and begin to deal with our fellowmen we drop the big words because we are more interested in making people understand us than we are in parading our learning. . . . If a young man used big words to assure his sweetheart of his affection, she would never understand him, but the word *love* has but one syllable, just as the words *life, faith, hope, home, food,* and *work* are one-syllable words. Remember that nearly every audience is made up of people who differ in the amount of book learning they have received. If you speak only to those best educated you will speak over the heads of those less educated. . . . If you use little words you can reach not only the least learned but the most learned as well.[9]

3. **Familiarity.** Not only must words be simple, they must also be familiar. Every speaker should strive to use words that are commonly used by the people to whom he is speaking. Words become "loaded" through long usage, and the speaker can well take advantage of this. For example, the word "home" is much more impelling than the word "house." "Play" is better than "amusement." "Think" is better than "reflect." "Mud" is better than "mire." Simple words of long usage are like familiar friends and add warmth to one's speaking.

4. **Exactness.** There is a tendency to use an "omnibus" word, or a kind of "cover-all," instead of the exact word. Everything becomes *beautiful,* whether it is a lake, a cow, a new car, a sunset, or a pretty girl. Instead of describing everything with general, overworked words, it is better in each case to choose a word that has the exact meaning that is required. A building can be: a hotel, a log cabin, a cathedral, a sky-

[9]Bryan, *In His Image*, p. 256.

scraper, a bungalow, a shed, a barn, a palace, and so on. Use the exact word.

5. **Good taste.** Public speaking needs to be more formal than ordinary conversation. This does not mean that it should be stilted, but simply that slang and loose expressions should be dropped. There are also certain "low-caste" words which are better left out of public address. For example, it is better to say "smell" than "stink," "food" than "chow," "cow" than "critter." There is never an occasion, public or otherwise, for the Christian to use profanity or vulgarity.

As you work on your style of speaking, be more conscious of the words that you, and others, use. Consciously try to increase your vocabulary so that you will have the right word for every situation. Wide reading, careful listening to cultured people, and the dictionary habit (looking up all new words heard or read) will accomplish much along this line in a reasonably short time. Remember that words are tools, and that you must have the right tools for public speaking.

REMEMBERING NAMES

Although names are not words in the usual sense, they are vitally important to anyone who speaks in public or who takes an active part in the Lord's work. Your work will be more efficient if you remember the names of the persons whom you meet. According to Carl Seashore, the psychologist, "The average man does not use above ten per cent of his actual inherited capacity for memory. He wastes the ninety per cent by violating the natural laws of remembering." These natural laws are: impression, repetition, and association. We have not the space for more than a few simple suggestions but these will pay big dividends if put into practice. The following rules are worth remembering:

1. **Learn the name accurately.** If you did not hear the name distinctly, say so immediately, and ask that it be repeated. A new acquaintance never minds giving his name a second time. He is complimented to think that you are interested in him.

2. **Repeat the name aloud.** While talking with him, try to use his name two or three times before you part, for this will stamp it into your memory, making it easier to recall later.

3. **Study the physical features.** While talking with the new acquaintance focus your attention for a few moments upon the outstanding physical features: hair, face, size, height, and other such characteristics. Try to remember something distinctive about the person.

4. **Associate the name with something.** Consciously connect the new name with a familiar idea or ideas. For example, when you meet Mr. Waldrop, think of a falling wall (wall drop). Mr. Green suggests the grass of your front lawn.

5. **Set down the name and the identifying details.** When convenient, set down on paper the new name. Attach to it the marks of identification referred to above. Writing it will stamp it in almost indelibly.

PRONUNCIATION

In addition to selecting the right words, you have the obligation as a speaker to pronounce them correctly. As you master new words and add them to your vocabulary, be sure that you also learn the correct pronunciation. Actually, some words have more than one correct pronunciation, for educated people in different sections of the country pronounce them differently. "Either" and "neither" are such words. The only safe procedure is to go to some generally accepted authority and check the pronunciation. Use the first pronunciation given unless you are certain that it is not commonly used by educated people of your area. In that case use the second or even the third pronunciation. The rule is, *pronounce your words as the best educated people in your community pronounce them.*

ACTIVITIES

1. Using a good pronouncing Bible check the pronunciation of all the books of the Bible, the leading geographical names, and the names of the leading characters. In the activity period of the class, practice aloud the correct pronunciation of these words. It might add interest to make a "pronouncing bee" of it, by dividing the class into competing teams. Be sure to pronounce *Jerusalem* without a *z*.

2. Listed below are carefully chosen words whose pronunciation you should know. Before coming to class, check the pronunciation of each word so that you know what is correct.

A. Pronounce with attention to vowels:

acquiesce	creek	gape
amen	crunch	garrulous
amenable	culinary	gaunt
apparatus	dais	granary
archive	denouement	gratis
bade	deprivation	harem
bestial	desperado	heinous
biography	docile	hilarious
bravado	drama	hypocrisy
brooch	employee	imbecile
cleanly	envelope	implacable
clematis	envoy	infantile
clique	epoch	inveigle
comely	equable	jocund
courier	equine	jowl
courtesy	fiancée	juvenile
courtier	forge	leisure
covert	gala	libertine

manor	plait	project (noun, verb)
maritime	predecessor	rabbi
mercantile	prelude	rout
oblique	process	senile
pageant	produce (noun, verb)	servile
pianist	profile	visor
placable	program	water
plaid	progress (noun, verb)	wound

B. Pronounce with attention to consonant sounds:

architect	February	licorice
arctic	forehead	loath
blackguard	gibberish	luxury
buffet	gibbet	oath
cognizance	gooseberry	poignant
column	height	pronunciation
concerto	hiccough	rhythm
corps	homage	soldier
credulity	improvisation	subpoena
desultory	incognito	thence
diphtheria	isthmus	thither
diphthong	jasmine	thyme
draught	kiln	wharf
drought	lambrequin	with
exit	lichen	wreath

C. Pronounce with attention to correct accent:

acclimate	cognomen	formidable
address	combatant	gondola
adult	commandant	grimace
alias	defect	hospitable
ally	despicable	impious
aspirant	explicable	indissoluble
chastisement	exquisite	inexorable

inquiry	pretext	routine
interesting	recall	theater
irreparable	recess	toward
irrevocable	research	vagary
lamentable	romance	

D. Pronounce with attention to syllabication:

accurate	film	neuralgia
annihilate	gaseous	nihilist
conduit	glacial	often
courteous	guardian	recognize
daguerreotype	heaven	remediable
décolleté	hieroglyphic	statistics
desuetude	lenient	subtle
evening	lineament	toward
every	lien	temperament
extraordinary	nausea	

E. Pronounce the following words, which are often confused:

accent	decade	quote
assent	decayed	coat
alumna	decease	soldier
alumnae	disease	solder
alumni	either	stature
adapt	ether	statute
adept	moral	statue
adopt	.morale	track
affect	formally	tract
effect	formerly	wander
broach	hospital	wonder
brooch	hospitable	pillar
cease	perquisite	pillow
seize	prerequisite	
courtesy		
curtsy		

CHAPTER XVI

What Next—Preaching?

AFTER THESE WEEKS given to learning the basic principles of good speaking, what are your responsibilities to the Lord? You have a greater obligation to help in the Lord's work than when you began the study, for you are better fitted to fill places of responsibility and leadership. Whether you have one talent or five, there is a worth-while work for you to do. In a sense you stand at the crossroads, for you will either slip back into inactivity, or move ahead into an ever increasing sphere of usefulness. Which way will you go?

Several years ago I visited the campus of a religious college in which some thirteen hundred students were enrolled. My guide explained that all these students were committed to giving several years of their lives to "full-time service to their Lord." They came from most of the forty-eight states and had been recruited for full-time religious service from a religious body numbering only 225,527 members. Obviously, this meant that the parents, teachers, and preachers in that denomination placed great emphasis on full-time religious work. This is part of the reason why it has representatives on all continents and in most countries of the world.

The only possible solution to the problem of a lost world is to be found in a greater number of workers. Of course it is fully understood that every Christian is to preach the Word; but the hard fact is that the average person who has to earn a living through secular employment, with the usual family responsibilities, has only a minimum of time left for the Lord's work. We need more *full-time workers.*

If not every person can give all his time to work for the Lord, who should be full-time workers? More specifically, who should preach? It is left to the careful judgment and reason of Christians to decide who shall become full-time evangelists. The following suggestions may help you to decide whether or not you should seriously consider becoming a preacher:

1. **Do you have a deep abiding faith in God, Christ, and the Bible?** It may seem to be unnecessary to state this requirement, but in a day of liberal theology and modernistic teaching it is the *only* foundation on which a life of preaching can be built. The "social gospel" and the "Oxford Group Movement" may be of some benefit to the world; but they do not save souls and are not the essential work that the evangelists and teachers of the New Testament period set out to do.

2. **Do you have a deep-seated desire to preach the gospel in order to save souls?** Many motives may cause a man to want to preach: the applause of fellow men, financial considerations, escape from military service are a few. The only worthy motive, however, is the urgent, overpowering desire to help others be saved. Many people question the sincerity of the preacher. Booker T. Washington, for instance, described the heat of the cotton patch, sweat running down the face and back, dust fogging up around the ankles, and in the midst of all of this the dropping of the hoe, the leaving of the field with the words, 'Brethren, I's called to preach." While there may be some who decide to preach in order to escape physical labor,

or Uncle Sam's draft call, the great overwhelming majority of those who preach are men of pure motives, dedicated lives, and deep convictions. So must it ever be.

3. **Do you have the qualifications for preaching?** It is a dangerous undertaking to list the essential qualifications for preaching, for there are many men who have rendered great service to the Lord though deficient in one or more of the usually necessary qualifications. Nevertheless, our list would include: (a) character, (b) sincerity, (c) a good mind, (d) knowledge, (e) enthusiasm, (f) courage, (g) originality, (h) health, (i) humility, and (j) ability to speak. Sometimes men with small qualifications do unbelievably effective work for the Lord. There was the young man whose beginning sermons seemed to be the least promising of any that we had heard, and for whom we had little hope as a preacher; but a year later he glowingly reported a meeting in which more than forty had responded to the invitation. There is a place for everyone who is willing to give himself to the Lord's work. Other things being equal, however, the man who has the greatest number of the above qualifications and has each to the highest degree will do the best work for the Lord. Henry Ward Beecher strikingly emphasized the need for first-rate abilities in the words:

When God calls very loud at the time you are born, standing at the door of life, and says, "Quarter of a man, come forth!" that man is not for the ministry. "Half a man, come forth!" no; that will not do for a preacher. "Whole man, come!" that is *you.* The man must be a man, and a full man, that is going to be a true Christian minister.[1]

4. **Do you have the encouragement of judicious friends?** Possibly no person can be objective enough to make the de-

---

[1]Beecher, *Yale Lectures on Preaching,* I, 40.

cision as to whether or not his life should be devoted to preaching, without the advice of others. Let those others be the most consecrated Christians that you know—elders, who have known you from childhood, Bible-class teachers, Christian parents, preachers who know something of the demands of the work.

5. **Do you have the cooperation of circumstances—indicating God's approval?** There are some who can be more valuable to the Lord as businessmen or schoolteachers or in other areas of work than in full-time preaching. Their greatest service would be as elders, deacons, or in some other phase of the Lord's work. When such a one mistakenly endeavors to preach full time, the Lord may indicate his wishes through the closing of doors. Likewise many a preacher of the gospel has felt the encouragement of the Lord through the opening of doors and in finding unexpected opportunities for service placed before him. We who believe in *divine providence* believe that the Lord helps his children decide where they can serve him best.

These are some of the considerations that should be carefully examined by those who would give themselves to full-time preaching of the gospel. Preaching is the greatest work in the world. It means some sacrifices, much hard work, and occasional disappointments, but it also means the greatest joy and satisfaction that this world knows. "Let him know, that he who converteth a sinner from the error of his way shall save a soul from death, and shall cover a multitude of sins."[2] Why not accept the divine challenge: "I charge thee in the sight of God and of Christ Jesus, who shall judge the living and the dead, and by his appearing and his kingdom: preach the word; be urgent in season, out of season; reprove, rebuke, exhort, with all longsuffering and teaching. . . . But be thou sober in all things, suffer hardship, do the work of an evangelist, fulfil thy ministry."[3] God had but one Son, and He was a preacher.

---

[2]James 5:20.   [3]II Timothy 4:1–2, 5.

Bibliography

Anderson, Virgil A., *Training the Speaking Voice*. New York: Oxford University Press, 1942. 387 pp.

Aristotle, *The Rhetoric of Aristotle,* translated by J. E. C. Welldon. London: Macmillan and Company, 1886. 306 pp.

Athenagoras. See Justin.

Baird, A. Craig, *Argumentation, Discussion, and Debate*. New York: McGraw-Hill Book Company, 1950. 422 pp.

———, editor, *Representative American Speeches, 1945–46*. New York: H. W. Wilson Company, 1946.

———, and Franklin H. Knower, *General Speech: An Introduction*. New York: McGraw-Hill Book Company, 1949. 500 pp.

Baxter, Batsell Barrett, *The Heart of the Yale Lectures*. New York: The Macmillan Company, 1947. 332 pp.

Beecher, Henry Ward, *Yale Lectures on Preaching,* 3 vols. New York: Fords, Howard & Hulbert, 1892.

Borchers, Gladys L., and Claude M. Wise, *Modern Speech*. New York: Harcourt, Brace and Company, 1947. 522 pp.

Borden, Richard C., *Public Speaking—As Listeners Like It!* New York: Harper & Brothers, 1935. 111 pp.

Brigance, William Norwood, *Classified Speech Models of Eighteen Forms of Public Address*. New York: F. S. Crofts & Co., 1928. 413 pp.

———, *Speech: Its Techniques and Disciplines in a Free Society*. New York: Appleton-Century-Crofts, 1952. 582 pp.

———, *Speech Composition*. New York: F. S. Crofts & Co., 1937. 385 pp.

———, and Ray Keeslar Immel, *Speechmaking: Principles and Practice*. New York: F. S. Crofts & Co., 1938. 385 pp.

Brooks, Phillips, *Lectures on Preaching*. New York: E. P. Dutton & Company, 1898. 281 pp.

Brown, Charles Reynolds, *The Art of Preaching*. New York: The Macmillan Company, 1922. 250 pp.

Bryan, William Jennings, *In His Image*. New York: Fleming H. Revell & Company, 1922. 266 pp.

Carnegie, Dale, *Public Speaking and Influencing Men in Business,* 2nd edition. New York: Association Press, 1937. 408 pp.

Conwell, Russell H., *Acres of Diamonds.* New York: Harper and Brothers, 1915. 59 pp.

Crosby, Howard, *The Christian Preacher.* New York: Anson D. F. Randolph & Company, 1879. 195 pp.

Curry, Samuel S., *Vocal and Literary Interpretation of the Bible.* New York: The Macmillan Company, 1903. 384 pp.

Dale, R. W., *Nine Lectures on Preaching.* London: Hodder & Stoughton, 1890. 302 pp.

Dewey, John, *How We Think.* Boston: D. C. Heath and Company, 1910. 224 pp.

Dixon, John, *How to Speak, Here, There, and on the Air.* New York: Abingdon-Cokesbury Press, 1949. 249 pp.

Eisenson, Jon, *The Psychology of Speech.* New York: F. S. Crofts & Co., 1938. 280 pp.

Emerson, Ralph Waldo, *Journals,* edited by Edward W. Emerson and Waldo E. Forbes, Vol. IX. Boston: Houghton Mifflin Company, 1914.

Gray, Giles Wilkeson, and Claude Merton Wise, *The Bases of Speech,* rev. ed. New York: Harper & Brothers, 1946. 610 pp.

Hedde, Wilhelmina G., and William Norwood Brigance, *American Speech,* 3rd ed. Philadelphia: J. B. Lippincott Company, 1951. 596 pp.

Holmes, Oliver Wendell, *The Autocrat of the Breakfast-Table.* Boston: Phillips, Sampson & Co., 1858.

Judson, Lyman Spicer, and Andrew Thomas Weaver, *Voice Science.* New York: F. S. Crofts & Co., 1942. 377 pp.

Justin Martyr and Athenagoras, *Writings,* translated by Marcus Dods, George Reith, and B. P. Pratten. Edinburgh: T. & T. Clark, 1868. 465 pp.

Lindgren, Homer D., editor, *Modern Speeches,* rev. ed. New York: F. S. Crofts & Co., 1930. 514 pp.

Lomas, Charles W., "Stage Fright," *Quarterly Journal of Speech,* 30:479–485 (Dec., 1944).

McBurney, James H., and Kenneth G. Hance, *The Principles and Methods of Discussion.* New York: Harper & Brothers, 1939. 452 pp.

Merrill, William Pierson, *The Freedom of the Preacher.* New York: The Macmillan Company, 1922. 147 pp.

Monroe, Alan H., *Principles and Types of Speech,* 3rd ed. Chicago: Scott, Foresman and Company, 1949. 658 pp.

Nichols, Alan, *Discussion and Debate.* New York: Harcourt, Brace and Company, 1941. 569 pp.

Nutt, Robert H., *How to Remember Names and Faces.* New York: Simon and Schuster, 1947. 247 pp.

Oliver, Robert T., Dallas C. Dickey, and Harold P. Zelko, *Essentials of Communicative Speech.* New York: The Dryden Press, 1949. 338 pp.

———, and Rupert L. Cortright, *New Training for Effective Speech,* rev. ed. New York: The Dryden Press, 1951. 563 pp.

Parrish, Wayland Maxfield, *Speaking in Public.* New York: Charles Scribner's Sons, 1947. 461 pp.

Phillips, Arthur Edward, *Effective Speaking,* new rev. ed. Chicago: The Newton Company, 1938. 384 pp.

Powers, David Guy, *Fundamentals of Speech.* New York: McGraw-Hill Book Company, 1951. 380 pp.

Reager, Richard C., *You Can Talk Well.* New Brunswick, N. J.: Rutgers University Press, 1946. 312 pp.

Sarett, Lew R., and William Trufant Foster, *Basic Principles of Speech,* rev. ed. Boston: Houghton Mifflin Company, 1946. 604 pp.

Scherer, Paul E., *For We Have This Treasure.* New York: Harper & Brothers, 1944. 212 pp.

Showalter, G. H. P., and Frank L. Cox, *A Book of Prayers.* Austin, Texas: Firm Foundation Publishing House, 1940. 94 pp.

Smith, Harley, Clara E. Krefting, and Ervin E. Lewis, *Everyday Speech.* New York: American Book Company, 1941. 479 pp.

Sockman, Ralph W., *The Highway of God.* New York: The Macmillan Company, 1942. 228 pp.

Taylor, William M., *The Ministry of the Word.* London: T. Nelson and Sons [1876]. 318 pp.

Thonssen, Lester W., *Selected Readings in Rhetoric and Public Speaking.* New York: The H. W. Wilson Company, 1942. 324 pp.

―――, and A. Craig Baird, *Speech Criticism.* New York: The Ronald Press Company, 1948. 542 pp.

―――, and Howard Gilkinson, *Basic Training in Speech,* 2nd ed. Boston: D. C. Heath and Company, 1953. 494 pp.

Van Riper, Charles, *Speech Correction.* New York: Prentice-Hall, 1939. 434 pp.

Watkins, Dwight Everett, Harrison M. Karr, and Zadie Harvey, *Stage Fright and What to Do About It.* Boston: Expression Company, 1940. 110 pp.

West, Robert W., Lou Kennedy, and Anna Carr, *The Rehabilitation of Speech.* New York: Harper & Brothers, 1937. 475 pp.

Winans, James A., *Speech-Making.* New York: D. Appleton-Century Company, 1938. 488 pp.

Yeager, Willard Hayes, *Effective Speaking for Every Occasion.* New York: Prentice-Hall, 1940. 444 pp.

Appendix A

CASE HISTORY QUESTIONNAIRE

Name_____Age_____
       LAST   FIRST   MIDDLE

Home address_____Phone_____

_____

PERSONAL HISTORY

High school attended_____

College attended_____

Service in the Armed Forces?_____

How much reading do you normally do? What do you read?_____

_____

_____

_____

What periodicals do you read regularly?_____

_____

What are your major interests?_____

_____

Where have you traveled?_____

_____

In what work are you employed?_____

_____

SPEECH HISTORY

Have you ever taken a course in speech before? _____ If so, give a brief
description of the contents of the course._____

_____

How much public-speaking experience have you had?_____

_____

_____

_____

Do you have any troublesome speech defect? _____ If so, describe it:

_____

_____

What do you hope to accomplish in this course?_____

_____

Appendix B

EVALUATION CHART FOR BRIEF SPEECHES

Name_____ Subject_____

	40	50	60	70	80	90	100
SELECTION OF SUBJECT							
CHOICE OF SUPPORTING MATERIAL							
ORGANIZATION							
GRAMMAR							
PRONOUNCIATION AND WORD CHOICE							
VOICE							
BODILY ACTION							
AUDIENCE CONTACT							
SPEECH ATTITUDE							
GENERAL EFFECTIVENESS							

Comments: Evaluation:

EVALUATION CHART FOR LONGER SPEECHES

Name _____ Date _____ Evaluation _____

Subject _____

VOICE	Excel.	Good	Aver.	Poor	Comments
1. QUALITY					
2. PITCH					
3. RATE					
4. FORCE					

ACTION	Excel.	Good	Aver.	Poor	Comments
1. PERSONAL APPEARANCE					
2. POSTURE					
3. GESTURES					
4. FACIAL EXPRESSION					
5. PLATFORM MOVEMENT					
6. MANNERISMS					

SUBJECT MATTER

1. Organization:

    a. Beginning: (　) Irrelevant; (　) Not Clear; (　) Too Long; (　) Failed to Capture Immediate Attention. Also:

    _____

    b. Body of the speech: (　) Rambling; (　) Illogical Arrangement of Ideas; (　) General Statements Not Properly Supported or Developed.

    Also: _____

    c. Ending: (　) Failed to Summarize; (　) Failed to Include Call for Action or Acceptance; (　) Vague; (　) Irrelevant; (　) Weak; (　) Lacked Climactic Effect. Also:

    _____

2. Material: (　) Indicated Lack of Preparation; (　) Lacked Authority; (　) Speaker Failed to Make Original Material Sufficiently His Own; (　) Poorly Adapted to Audience; (　) Dull; (　) General; (　) Poorly Suited to Speaker's Capacity; (　) Irrelevant to Topic. Also:

_____

DICTION

1. Words Mispronounced
2. Errors in Grammar
3. Words Misused

MISCELLANEOUS COMMENTS: